Stopping the Buck

Selections from
From the States

Edited by Peter T. Ewell

Assessment
UPdate
COLLECTIONS

Published by Jossey-Bass
A Wiley Imprint
989 Market Street, San Francisco, CA 94103-1741   www.josseybass.com

Jossey-Bass books and products are available through most bookstores. To contact Jossey-Bass directly call our Customer Care Department within the U.S. at 800-956-7739, outside the U.S. at 317-572-3986, or fax 317-572-4002.

Jossey-Bass also publishes its books in a variety of electronic formats. Some content that appears in print may not be available in electronic books.

Library of Congress Cataloging-in-Publication Data available upon request

FIRST EDITION
PB Printing   10 9 8 7 6 5 4 3 2 1

Contents

INTRODUCTION

Stopping the Buck:
Selections from
"From the States"

When *Assessment Update* was launched in the spring of 1989, "From the States" was intended to review the many state assessment mandates that were rapidly being put in place at that time. Since that time, I have gradually broadened the column's scope to include additional topics that bear on the connection between assessment and accountability, embracing federal developments, the accreditation scene, and occasional forays abroad. As I pulled together the columns to include in this collection, moreover, I was struck by the way state and federal authorities have steadily increased their footprint in academic affairs, primarily through the mechanism of assessment. Reflecting on this, I recalled a quote from Harold Enarson in a *Change Magazine* article many years ago (October, 1980, p. 9) that underscores the dispersal of authority, and hence the uncertainty, wrought by external forces on colleges and universities: "when no one is in charge, no one is fully accountable … I could once say decisively 'the buck stops here'… now it never stops." "Stopping the buck"—or at least taking a snapshot of where things stand with respect to accountability and assessment—is thus a good way to characterize what I have been up to in this column for the past two decades.

During that time, the relevant accountability actors motivating assessment have shifted markedly. States indeed initiated the assessment/accountability conversation, and it is fair to claim that had this not occurred, assessment as we know it would not be around today. More than two-thirds of the states had mandated assessment by 1990 when the first systematic inventory was taken by the Education Commission of the States. This is the period for the most part covered by the first section of this collection. But faced with budget shortfalls, state efforts quickly peaked. At least as important, institutions responded unevenly to the initial set of mandates, with some being proactive and creative, and others resisting. As predicted in my initial column, one result was successive rebounds in accountability pressure over the years. In the 1990s, as described in this collection's second section, states began a veritable romance with statistical performance indicators, putting a harder edge on accountability for public institutions extending far beyond learning outcomes assessment. Meanwhile, the main source of pressure for assessment itself increasingly moved from states to regional accreditors. This meant that all institutions, not just public institutions, had to get involved. And standing behind the accreditors was the federal government, harnessing the connection between accredited status and institutional eligibility to receive federal funds to make sure that everybody was paying attention to assessment. These developments, culminating with the Secretary's Commission on the Future of Higher Education (popularly known as the "Spellings Commission") in 2006, are the territory covered by this collection's third and final section.

Finally, readers should always bear in mind when perusing this material that these columns "stop the buck" at particular points in time, so the observations I offer in each are confined to that context. This makes this collection a bit different from its companions in the *Assessment Update* series because it offers no enduring wisdom. Its principal lesson is that of any history: awareness of past mistakes is one key to avoiding them in the future.

State-Level Assessment (1989–1998)

An initial review of state activities constituted the first "From the States," with one state effort reviewed in each of several subsequent columns published in the newsletter's first five years. The first section of this collection consists of excerpts from this initial column describing the state of play at that time, followed by six examples of columns devoted to a single state, then a column examining two of them a few years later after the country had experienced a recession, together with a column at the end of the period when standardized testing was once again coming into fashion.

Introduction to the Series

From Assessment Update *1:1 (1989).*

In this initial issue, I will quickly sketch the current pattern of state assessment initiatives. A first and reasonable question is how many there are. Obviously any count depends on how the question is framed. In its follow-up to "Time for Results," for example, the National Governors' Association reports only thirteen states without an assessment program either "in place or under consideration." ACE's "Campus Trends" survey for 1988 paints a different picture: 29 percent of institutional respondents report that their state "is currently requiring assessment procedures." Clearly, a count of these initiatives depends on definition.

My own personal count of about fifteen states is based on the following criteria: (1) the existence of a formal document, enabling legislation, executive order, or board resolution on assessment; (2) an identifiable staff assignment or budget line for the program; and (3) a distinct and concrete requirement that institutions report progress or results. This count represents three more states than a year ago—a clear addition, but by no means the runaway train predicted by some. My best guess is that this rate of growth will remain steady for the foreseeable future—that is, another two or three states probably can be expected to mandate something each year.

Another question commonly posed is whether the character of state assessment initiatives is changing. Here the answer is definitely yes. First, in contrast to initial mandates that often had their origins in the state house or governor's mansion, the newer initiatives are coming from governing and coordinating boards. The past year saw no new legislation on assessment of the character of Colorado's HB1187 or Texas's SB543. Legislative action, if present at all, has occurred in response to board request. This trend indicates an important seizure of the initiative by system governing and coordinating boards and may significantly affect what is requested of institutions. On the one hand, institutions can probably expect assessment mandates to be better adapted to institutional realities; on the other hand, there also may be a greater tendency for assessment to be treated in familiar fashion by state agencies—as primarily a bureaucratic reporting requirement.

Finally, state mandates continue to emphasize institutional initiative. Their modal tendency is to require institutions to develop assessment plans covering such areas as basic skills and remediation, general education, achievement in the major field, student satisfaction, and alumni placement and achievement, with a fairly open-ended set of guidelines. Generally, institutions are required to report progress in implementing their plans on an annual basis. In addition, beginning in the second or third year of implementation, most guidelines require institutions to report results in summary form, together with a description of actions taken locally to improve effectiveness.

All told, the picture is one in which individual institutions retain considerable discretion—if they choose to exercise it. At the same time, institutions will continue to have many opportunities to help shape state requirements that have not been fully nailed down. But they are well advised to act quickly. As a consequence of seizing the initiative, state boards are under increasing pressure to show action. And without a credible institutional response, they may show considerably less flexibility than has been the case up to now.

Assessment in Virginia: A State Profile

From Assessment Update *1:1 (1989).*

The origins of Virginia's assessment initiative date back almost four years to the publication of NIE's report *Involvement in Learning*. After reading this report, several Virginia legislators were persuaded that some kind of assessment was needed to ensure quality. At the time, several states, most prominently Florida and Tennessee, had already mandated statewide testing, and Virginia legislators initially were inclined to follow suit. But they were quickly persuaded by the State Council for Higher Education in Virginia (SCHEV), the state's higher education coordinating body, to propose a study resolution instead. In 1986, the Council completed its study, and using it as a guide, the legislature mandated that each of the state's public higher education institutions develop its own plan to assess the outcomes of undergraduate education to be submitted to the Council for approval. Plans were to be submitted by June 1987 and were prepared within general guidelines established by the Council and a committee of institutional representatives. A strong inducement for institutions to cooperate was provided by a link between plan approval and access to state incentive funding: if an acceptable plan were not provided, the governor would not recommend institutions for such funds.

By 1987, each institution in Virginia had an approved assessment plan that is now in the process of being implemented. True to the spirit of the program, Virginia institutions have developed a range of diverse, often innovative, assessment approaches, supported by a total of $4.4 million in state funds allocated to institutions for local assessment purposes over the 1988–1990 biennium. Beginning in July 1989, institutions will be required to report information within the categories established by the guidelines—outcomes in the major and general education, basic skills proficiency and the effectiveness of remediation, and alumni follow-up. In each of these categories, institutions are to present summaries of the results obtained, describe their reliability and validity, analyze what they mean, and describe any institutional action taken as a result.

By counting heavily upon institutional initiative, Virginia's assessment approach has been called both exemplary and risky. Certainly it allows for considerable flexibility in the ways institutions can approach the task of building assessment. Emerging programs at James Madison University, George Mason University, Longwood College, the College of William and Mary, and many others are innovative and are tailored to the mission, clientele, and culture of each institution. Such programs provide evidence that, given proactive local leadership, such a program can work. But the Virginia approach is also risky. Banking heavily on institutional initiative first carries with it the substantial possibility of uneven response. Some institutions will be proactive, while others may do little or nothing. What to do about the latter remains a compelling problem for SCHEV. Second, there is a potential problem in using the resulting information for accountability purposes. Virginia's approach is premised on the proposition that accountability and academic improvement need not be in conflict and that programs that result in improvement also will serve to demonstrate effectiveness to the legislature and the public. Much, therefore, depends upon the State Council's ability in the coming year to translate a necessarily diverse and noncomparable set of institutional assessment reports into policy information that will satisfy the legislature and the public.

Because of these features, I believe that events in Virginia should be watched closely in the coming year. Many states now debating the best assessment approach will be interested in both the overall quality of programs built by Virginia institutions and the degree to which external constituencies in Virginia are satisfied with the information provided. How Virginia fares may help determine the shape of assessment in many other states.

Assessment in New Jersey: A State Profile

From Assessment Update *1:2 (1989).*

New Jersey's College Outcomes Evaluation Program (COEP) is probably the most extensive, visible, and proactive initiative in the current new wave of state assessment mandates. Considerable resources, strong support from Governor Thomas Kean and the legislature, and active leadership from the state's Department of Higher Education (DHE) combine in New Jersey to provide an unprecedented range of activities. New Jersey's effort also has an unusually long time horizon. Formally launched in 1985, the program's complete implementation extends into the 1990s. New Jersey's program is both more systematic and more centralized than other state initiatives; multiple statewide task forces actively led and supported by DHE produced an extensive set of guidelines and procedures. At the same time, high levels of central coordination and support rendered conceivable the development of some common statewide measurement initiatives.

In 1985, Chancellor T. Edward Hollander outlined a set of principles and guidelines for a program stressing the use of assessment information for instructional improvement. Two years of deliberation by a 23-member COEP advisory committee, consisting of faculty and administrators from across the state, shaped a program adopted in 1987. It included a common statewide general intellectual skills examination, based on a new technology of cognitive assessment, and a range of local evaluation activities, to be carried out by each institution. COEP's first component broke new ground in at least two ways. While a number of states—among them Florida, Georgia, South Dakota, and Tennessee—had previously developed common postsecondary testing programs, none had chosen the difficult route of building its own examination designed explicitly for comprehensive program evaluation. As a result, the coverage of the New Jersey examination is distinctive—an identifiable set of cross-cutting collegiate skills, described in terms of "gathering, analyzing, and presenting information." Second, the proposed examination, while standardized, is not based on such traditional recall-based methods as multiple choice. Instead, its core consists of a series of judgmentally scored tasks requiring students to comprehend, manipulate, and communicate complex bodies of information. To develop the required instrument, DHE contracted with the Educational Testing Service (ETS) to work with faculty teams in 1987–1988. Initial tryouts of task-based items took place in the spring of 1988, and full-scale pilot tests were under way at approximately a dozen campuses throughout the 1988–1989 academic year.

Under COEP's other components, institutions in New Jersey are developing their own procedures for assessing the effectiveness of instruction in general education and major fields, and of assessing students' personal development, satisfaction, and behavior after college. Local evaluation processes also address faculty, research, and creative activity, as well as the institution's impact on the community and society. Institutions submitted progress reports on their implementation of these activities in June 1988 and will report initial results in 1989. Rather than providing institutions with a simple set of assessment guidelines, as in Virginia or Colorado, New Jersey's approach gives campuses substantial advice about appropriate methodologies, in the form of specially prepared manuals, literature reviews, and accompanying workshops.

These documents summarize the available techniques, approaches, and background literature related to a particular assessment area, in a form suitable for use by local practitioners. Information produced by local assessment is also supplemented by data drawn from available statewide databases.

Overall, COEP constitutes an instructive and distinctive field experiment of assessment practice that must overcome some formidable risks to be successful. Because of proactive leadership, state policymakers are incurring the risk that the effort will be perceived by institutions as a top-down initiative, lacking visible mechanisms for inducing institutional ownership and response. Technical risks involved in developing and fielding the general intellectual skills examination are also daunting. Because of its task-based approach, the instrument must overcome significant challenges with respect to scoring, the reliability of obtained results, and the great unknown of student motivation.

But the potential payoffs of New Jersey's assessment approach are also considerable. For New Jersey, COEP has the potential to provide policymakers with a comprehensive common database in terms of which to concretely demonstrate the state's return on investment in higher education. For the rest of us, COEP's pioneering task-based general intellectual skills examination represents an excellent alternative to large-scale multiple-choice testing. If it is successful, we will no doubt soon see versions of this technology marketed by ETS and others. Similarly, New Jersey's careful process of instrument and method review has produced a set of documents useful to any institution contemplating assessment; the COEP advisory committee's report alone is a valuable primer of assessment practice.

COEP represents a major test case for state-based assessment. A massive effort, clear political support, and a long timeline imply that if the initiative fails to achieve its political objectives here, it is unlikely to succeed anywhere else. All told, over the next few years New Jersey will be an interesting place to watch.

Assessment in Florida: Review of the CLAST Testing Program

From Assessment Update *1:3 (1989)*.

Probably the best-known current example of statewide assessment is Florida's College-Level Academic Skills Testing (CLAST) program. The roots of CLAST date from 1973, when Florida began a major effort to upgrade its educational systems through direct state action. Rapid population growth, consequent increases in state budgets, and strong political support from both the legislature and the governor all contributed to a favorable climate for a proactive state role. CLAST's immediate impetus was a trial competency test of teachers in the St. Petersburg region, which obtained disappointing results.

Reinforced by concerns about grade inflation and other issues in teacher education programs, the mood of the legislators and the governor was favorable for extending the state's growing K–12 competency testing movement into higher education.

Initiated on a voluntary basis in 1979, with considerable faculty participation, the program's initial task was to define and assess a relatively narrow range of essential academic skills, including reading, writing, and computation. By 1982, an instrument was ready for general use. It was designed primarily at Florida State University under the guidance of numerous statewide committees, and the first official scores were to have been recorded in 1984. Beginning in that year, students would be substantially barred from junior-level coursework if they had not passed CLAST after three attempts.

Because of its high-stakes nature CLAST was immediately controversial and has remained so. Adverse minority impacts and widespread perceptions of "teaching to the test" are particular concerns. In both cases, attention has centered on community colleges; the vast majority of four-year college students can easily pass the examination at current standards. While both objections have some merit, the case is far from decisive. Overall pass rates on CLAST have averaged 95% after three tries over the last several years, with black and Hispanic pass rates at 87% and 92%, respectively. In general, student performance has kept pace with rising standards.

Vocal opponents of CLAST, such as Miami-Dade Community College, have claimed significant adverse impacts as a result of testing (for example, substantial declines, particularly among minorities, among students enrolling in AA transfer degree programs). Other institutions, in contrast, have claimed positive impacts in the form of needed curricular realignment and more uniform standards. All institutions, moreover, have benefited from the additional funds appropriated by the legislature to implement CLAST reforms.

Most state policymakers currently see CLAST as having accomplished its original and rather narrowly defined objectives; consequently, they are not inclined to extend the program. Moreover, Florida's ten-year effort to reform higher education through direct state action now appears to be losing its momentum. A new and less supportive administration is in office, and level state budgets are expected over the next few years. For CLAST, these changes are most visible in a recent proposal to delay implementation of higher 1989 pass-rate standards. While the political issue of adverse minority impact is real, the main reason for considering delay was to rethink the state's strategy for assessment and reform. Although the 1989 standards were eventually implemented as planned, many continue to question whether there is too much testing in Florida and, by implication, too much "micromanagement" of institutions.

Despite current fashion, observers of assessment should be particularly cautious about generalizing the experience of CLAST to other states and should remember that Florida's testing program was intended to achieve very limited ends. Thoughtfully inspected, however, the CLAST experience can provide many lessons about how best to initiate and respond to a statewide initiative.

Assessment in Colorado:
A State Profile

From Assessment Update *1:4 (1989)*.

Colorado remains one of the few states where an assessment program was initiated by the legislature. In 1985, the Colorado General Assembly passed the Statewide Accountability Act (HB1187), requiring each of the state's 28 public institutions of higher education to be "held accountable for demonstrable improvements in student knowledge, capacities, and skills between entrance and graduation." In addition to citing cognitive development, the language of HB1187 noted additional dimensions of potential student development, including "self-confidence, persistence, leadership, empathy, social responsibility, and understanding of cultural and intellectual differences." To ensure compliance, the bill authorized the Colorado Commission on Higher Education (CCHE), beginning in July 1990, to withhold up to 2% of the operating appropriation of any institution failing to implement the bill's provisions.

Despite HB1187's directive language and strong penalties, the essence of Colorado's assessment approach is decentralized. No statewide instruments are mandated, and institutions are given considerable discretion to define their own assessment approaches. In designing the bill, Senator Al Meiklejohn, its sponsor, was thinking explicitly about the accountability process required of Colorado's elementary and secondary schools—largely a public self-study, with considerable local community input and involvement. One element of Meiklejohn's intent was to stimulate local improvement in this way; another was to send an unambiguous signal to higher education that its responsiveness was also required.

From the beginning, CCHE encountered difficulties in developing guidelines for institutional plans. The fact that most assessment elements were written explicitly into the law severely limited CCHE's maneuvering room. HB1187 also redefined CCHE as a strong statewide coordinating board, authorizing it to establish mandatory institutional admissions requirements, to discontinue duplicative programs, and to establish a statewide funds-for-excellence program. Short of staff, CCHE had little choice but to implement such provisions piecemeal, with their priorities dictated by the target dates specified in law.

CCHE's new responsibilities also raised wider governance issues. Unlike the State Council in Virginia or the Department of Higher Education in New Jersey, which may negotiate directly with institutions on the development of assessment policy, CCHE has to work through the state's five separate governing boards. One result was further delay in implementation and, more important, impediments to the kind of direct communication necessary to prevent misunderstanding. Finally, no new funds were earmarked for assessment; institutions were expected to pay for their own programs with existing resources.

Institutional responses were required in two stages. In June 1988, institutions submitted statements of their goals and objectives for undergraduate education. Full-scale assessment plans were required the following December. While this sequence was conceptually sound, many faculty were more opposed to the implication that the state could legitimately approve instructional goals than they were to assessment. At the same time, the 2% budget penalty rendered plan approval a high-stakes process. As in Virginia, the state's strategy was to enhance credibility by involving external consultants in the review. Unlike what happened in Virginia, however, institutions were visibly ranked for comparison purposes. Seven of 28 submitted plans were not approved until July 1989.

As in most states that follow a decentralized approach, assessment plans in Colorado differ widely. Approximately half the plans propose administering at least one nationally normed standardized general education examination. Others concentrate on major-field assessment, usually embedded in a new capstone course or senior seminar. All propose an array of student surveys and student retention studies. Few, however, indicate how assessment is to be locally coordinated or supported. More important, few indicate how the results obtained will be used locally to make improvements.

Because of its legislative origins, negative sanctions, and bureaucratic implementation, assessment in Colorado appears largely compliance-driven. It remains to be seen whether a majority of institutions can convert programs initiated under such circumstances into viable mechanisms for internal revitalization.

Assessment in South Dakota: A State Profile

From Assessment Update *2:1 (1990).*

The story of assessment in South Dakota illustrates many of the dynamics of any state initiative. Begun as an accountability mechanism, the program has evolved into a campus-centered effort, intended primarily for local instructional improvement

In 1984, the South Dakota Board of Regents adopted Resolution 32-1984 requiring all six public four-year institutions to engage in a program modeled on Northeast Missouri State University's value-added approach. General education was to be assessed through a test-retest process for entering freshmen and second-semester sophomores, using the ACT Assessment and the Objective Form of the ACT-COMP. In addition, all graduating seniors were required to take nationally normed examinations in their major fields. Test scores would not be used to bar students from graduation nor would they be made a part of their permanent records. To support the effort, the resolution stipulated, students would be charged an additional fee.

Not surprisingly, statewide testing was not warmly received at the campus level. Although intrigued in the abstract by the emerging concept of assessment, administrators and faculty alike were apprehensive about a board-mandated program. Fees to pay for tests unrelated to their programs rankled many students and exacerbated already serious motivation problems. As the board sought to overcome growing resistance, a number of compromises emerged. First, the initial testing program was cut back—particularly in its major field areas: testing in the spring of 1985 was limited to the NTE exam in education, the EIT exam in engineering, and selected GRE major field examinations. More important, to meet fears about public disclosure and inappropriate comparison, the board agreed to a three-year moratorium on releasing obtained scores.

Perhaps the most significant move, however, was formation of a statewide testing committee with representatives drawn from each campus. The committee's role was crucial in the program's first three years—both in solving substantial day-to-day problems of implementation and in gradually evolving a more comprehensive, improvement-based concept of assessment as the program's prime intent.

By mid-1987, it was clear that the notion of statewide testing needed a second look. Inflexible test dates, high costs, and inadequate staff for data analysis all severely limited the utility of the data obtained, and made for nearly unworkable administration. In its June 1987 report to the board, the committee recommended major changes to simplify the program and to allow participating campuses greater flexibility.

Ownership of assessment moved from the regents to the campuses, and the content of the mandate shifted from requiring individual testing of all students to requiring that instructional programs be systematically evaluated by their own institutions. The newly developed program, launched in 1987–1988, continued to require assessment of common areas such as general education, the major field, student satisfaction, and basic skills/remediation. But consistent with emerging practice in other states, it allowed for considerable institutional discretion in selecting instruments and approaches.

For South Dakota this policy turnaround has produced the pattern of uneven development typical of most campus-centered state approaches. Some institutions have moved ahead quickly to develop vital, innovative approaches based on locally developed (often qualitative) instruments and techniques; here the program has shown important curricular and policy benefits. Others continue to administer and report on the standardized tests originally mandated. A parallel result has been an evolution of state purposes in assessment toward a more integrated, comprehensive evaluation effort embracing program review, enrollment analysis, and support for accreditation. Both, most observers feel, have been positive developments.

But state leaders should not be too quick to dismiss South Dakota's adventure with testing as without policy benefit. Board and campus representatives agree that their experience with statewide testing, though ultimately negative, helped mobilize initial interest in assessment, provided an occasion for serious ongoing discussion, and helped crystallize conclusions about what a good program might look like.

Assessment in Tennessee: A State Profile

From Assessment Update *2:3 (1990).*

Tennessee's Performance Funding Program, formally initiated in 1979, remains one of the most distinctive and most often cited approaches to state-based assessment. Simple in concept, its "reward for performance" features have made it attractive to legislators in many states who are seeking ways to improve the quality, responsiveness, and accountability of public colleges and universities. To date, however, no similar programs have emerged in other states.

The roots of what was initially called the Instructional Evaluation Schedule in Tennessee go back to the mid 1970s, when the state's higher education coordinating body—the Tennessee Higher Education Commission (THEC)—faced the familiar problem of justifying new funding in the context of shrinking enrollments. The idea of setting aside a limited amount of additional money to encourage better performance was highly attractive politically, both because it supported necessary appropriations and because it linked new dollars with a tangible return on investment. In contrast to much later assessment programs in other states, the Performance Funding Program was never really seen as a method of encouraging grassroots institutional change, but rather as a means of supporting necessary budget increases.

Because the program evolved slowly, there was time for significant campus involvement and gradual escalation of the stakes. From 1976 to 1979, the program operated as a pilot. In 1979, the legislature awarded the first funds for instructional evaluation activities in Tennessee's public institutions. By 1982, the shape of an operational program had emerged: set-aside funds would amount to 2% (later increased to 5%) of available instructional dollars statewide, and institutions would be allocated these funds on the basis of five performance criteria. Despite the *performance* label, only two of the five criteria—"value added" on the newly developed ACT-COMP examination and major-field testing with standardized exams—relied on actual test results. Two more—accrediting all accreditable programs and surveying students on their satisfaction—rewarded institutions just for engaging in the assessment process. The fifth criterion was based on the degree to which institutions actually used this information to make local improvements.

Despite initial doubts and opposition, most institutions adapted reasonably quickly to the new program. Some, including the University of Tennessee at Knoxville, made effective use of the leverage it provided to significantly enhance their own local assessment, planning, and program-review activities. By the end of the initial five-year authorization period, however, many were "topping out" on the process-oriented criteria, and THEC moved to realize the program's original performance-based design.

New performance-funding guidelines, issued in 1988 and currently in use, emphasize assessment results. For general education, the ACT-COMP has been retained, although institutions now earn performance-funding dollars both for score gains and for the absolute level of scores obtained. Dollar allocations in major fields are now based on actual test performance. Moreover, to ensure equitable performance judgments in the area of alumni satisfaction, a set of common statewide survey questions was developed, and results are used to allocate funds.

The merits and drawbacks of these changes, widely debated in Tennessee, are instructive for all other states and institutions. On the one hand, the new guidelines are considerably less ambiguous in their application, an important consideration when dollars are at stake. On the other hand, institutional observers see score-based performance criteria as inherently antithetical to developing the kind of faculty involvement most likely to produce instructional improvement.

On balance, however, performance funding in Tennessee is seen as a successful venture. From the THEC perspective, a major benefit is enhanced ability to talk effectively to the legislature. "It's very impressive when you don't just lead with a funding request," emphasizes the current THEC executive director. "The presence of these dollars helps us sell the rest of the budget." At the institutional level, moreover, the program has clearly provided incentives to develop a local assessment process that would otherwise not have gotten off the ground.

But both constituencies can also cite some unanticipated costs. Legislators concerned about higher education increasingly recognize that the logic of rewarding success, while compelling, may direct money away from the problems where it is most needed. In part, this motivation underlies a newer "legislative goals" initiative in Tennessee, whose purpose is less tied to rewarding performance. Institutional leaders have found that the existing performance-funding criteria may unintentionally be strengthening the hand of "sectional" curricular interests, particularly where national exams are available or where professional accreditation is at stake. As one campus administrator summarized the situation, "I'm worried about institutions feeling constrained by performance funding into doing things that lack local utility. . . . Maybe in this case you shouldn't go after these funds." In part, it is these attributes that have deterred other states from emulating Tennessee's assessment experiment.

Nevertheless, many of us continue to learn a great deal from Tennessee. As part of a pioneering venture, Tennessee's assessment efforts have been unusually well documented. As a result, they have effectively informed much of current assessment practice at both state and institutional levels.

Assessment in Hard Times: A Tale of Two States

From Assessment Update *4:1 (1992).*

In 1986, New Jersey and Virginia emerged as front-runners in the new game of state-based assessment. Both mounted generously funded, well-planned efforts, and in the coming years both would achieve substantial recognition for their alternative policy models (see this column in the Spring and Summer 1989 issues). Now, both states are in deep financial trouble. And how assessment has fared in each is worth a second look.

New Jersey's approach took the high road. Centered on the controversial and innovative General Intellectual Skills (GIS) examination, the state's College Outcomes Evaluation Program (COEP) remains unchallenged as the most comprehensive state-level assessment initiative attempted to date. From the outset, the program encountered substantial campus opposition—principally centered on the GIS exam. Indeed, for most participants, the GIS *was* COEP, despite the program's far more extensive (and campus-centered) components embracing student learning in general education and the major field, student development, research and creative activity, and campus contribution to the community.

Also unsettling for many campuses was the perception that COEP was part of an overall strategy for change on the part of the state's Department of Higher Education. While this approach promised campus leaders greater resources and the flexibility to manage them effectively, it also demanded greater accountability, and much of the available new funding was being invested in state-run categorical programs rather than being built into each institution's base. By 1989, increasing budget pressures made this strategy problematic. Resulting staff cutbacks at the department also rendered the original COEP design infeasible: remaining staff were unable to react to an increasing volume of campus reports or to further encourage local assessment development. The cornerstone of the program was seen to be the GIS exam, and all remaining resources were concentrated on putting it into place.

The eventual implementation of GIS in the spring of 1990 (after three years of development) was a technical triumph but a mixed success politically. Resources to support its first administration were denied by the legislature but were obtained from the governor's contingency fund. Several campuses boycotted the program and others complied under protest. Despite these difficulties, over 4,300 examinations were administered and scored and the results publicly reported. Much, however, had depended on strong departmental leadership and solid gubernatorial support. With a change of both in 1991, the program's future became doubtful. Again the legislature refused to fund the program, and this time the decision was made to suspend it.

While GIS was administered as planned in the spring of 1991, results were withheld—partly for budgetary reasons but probably also because their content was politically unpalatable. COEP is now officially "on hold"; some department officials want to revive it if times get better, but the program's rebirth in its original form is improbable. Meanwhile, campus-based assessment in New Jersey never really got started, and in the absence of a strong locally centered reporting mandate, many incipient programs themselves fell victim to budget cuts in 1989–1991.

Virginia, meanwhile, had taken a different road. In 1987, prompted by the legislature, the State Council on Higher Education (SCHEV) required each campus to develop its own assessment plan. While broad guidelines were provided, institutions were encouraged to adopt assessment approaches that best fit their missions, curricula, and student clienteles. On approval by the council, institutions were granted additional resources to implement their plans—resources that were later built into each institution's base allocation. Each biennium thereafter, institutions were required to report results comprehensively, addressing methods used, what was found, and what actions were taken as a result.

SCHEV's plan was also controversial, despite its campus-centered approach. Institutions complained about insufficient resources and short timelines for response, and in a state where institutional autonomy is the prevailing culture, they were also profoundly suspicious of state motives. But by the end of 1987, each had a plan in place and resources dedicated to carrying it out. Subsequent biennial reports to SCHEV in 1989 and 1991 revealed uneven response but for the most part a slow and steady progress in building a set of credible local processes.

By the end of 1989, Virginia was also facing severe budgetary problems, affecting state assessment policy in at least two ways. First, the decision to include assessment funds in each institution's base meant that institutional leaders were tempted to reallocate these funds to higher local priorities. Fear of this kind of response was precisely why state officials in New Jersey had decided on a far more directive approach in the first place. At the same time, the immense diversity of campus assessment activities made it hard for SCHEV to communicate exactly what assessment dollars were buying. SCHEV dealt with the first condition by privately, but severely, warning campus leaders off this course of action—recalling their ultimate authority to deny campuses access to discretionary funding in the absence of an "approved" assessment program. The second is a continuing problem.

Comparing the two states' approaches, Virginia's has certainly proven the more robust. While on many (and perhaps even a majority of) Virginia campuses assessment is still struggling, state action in many cases has proven an effective stimulus for gradually developing a valued and valuable local program.

It is useful to speculate what might have occurred had New Jersey's COEP enjoyed two or three additional years of generous funding and political goodwill. With the GIS exam in place, state priorities might have given more attention to local assessment concerns and to linking GIS results with statewide improvement efforts. As it happened, linkages to action and reform came too late to show the real utility of assessment, both to legislators and to campus leaders. But equally tempting when hard times hit might have been a proposal to use GIS results for "performance funding," a concept now enjoying something of a renaissance among state officials. In politics, some have said, timing is everything. It's an observation that seems particularly germane these days for those involved in state assessment policy.

Statewide Testing: The Sequel

From Assessment Update *10:5 (1998).*

When states began jumping on the mandated assessment bandwagon in the mid-to-late eighties, the first option proposed was always standardized testing. The reasons were many but always included legislative familiarity with standardized assessments in K–12, ease of acquisition, and the immediate public credibility that accompanies any instrument presumed to be valid and reliable. Counterarguments from higher education institutions in this period were vehement and predictable. More important, they were largely successful in diverting most mandates toward institution-centered approaches. Instead of forcing all institutions to adopt a single instrument through which their relative standings could be compared, colleges and universities were in most cases given the freedom to select their own assessment methods, as long as they did so responsibly, and publicly reported the results they obtained. Prominent milestones during this time of troubles were Washington's large-scale study of existing standardized tests in general education, which rejected all available alternatives as unsuitable; New Jersey's innovative College Outcomes Evaluation Program, which replaced multiple-choice tests with authentic (but expensive) task-based assessments; and South Dakota's abandonment of statewide general education testing as politically ineffective after three years. By the early nineties—with more than two thirds of the states in the assessment business—only a handful maintained a standardized testing program; among these stalwarts, moreover, were states such as Florida, Tennessee, and Georgia, which launched programs well before assessment became an accountability fashion, and undertook them for quite different policy reasons.

Lately, however, statewide standardized testing has been staging a comeback. In 1996, for instance, South Dakota again reversed its position, requiring all students to take the ACT-CAAP test. Similar and somewhat older programs in Arkansas and Wisconsin also use the CAAP. Most recently and visibly, this spring the State University of New York (SUNY) system and the Utah Board of Regents declared strong interests in establishing standardized testing programs for accountability purposes—in the former case, even issuing a widely circulated request for proposal (RFP) to assessment providers before a decision was made. Four of five of these initiatives emanate from governing boards rather than from coordinating boards (the source of the Arkansas initiative) or legislatures. All five make clear their intent to judge institutions comparatively; unlike Texas or Florida, for instance, no states, except South Dakota, will use test results to affect the fates of individual students. Finally, all five states make no bones about using off-the-shelf instruments; the SUNY RFP, for instance, requests that providers propose programs that can be fielded quickly by explicitly specifying the use of existing tests.

What lies behind this growing level of interest and activity? One part of the explanation is that institutional accountability measures in general—chiefly in the form of performance indicators—have grown sharply in popularity across the states. At least twenty states now report such statistics annually for all public institutions, and about eight reward high-scoring institutions directly with performance or incentive funds. With the exception of Tennessee, however, few states have actually used the results of outcomes testing to allocate funds. Some of the reasons for this anomaly were captured succinctly in national surveys conducted by NCHEMS and the University of Michigan in 1996–1997: although most state officials wanted outcomes testing as part of their performance-measure systems, at the time of these surveys few were ready to bear the fiscal and political price of trying to implement a large-scale testing program. With state budgets now bouncing back, accountability as salient as ever, and a new breed of substantially more aggressive incumbents sitting on state higher education boards, these restraining conditions are rapidly evaporating.

The new breed of politicians involved in these decisions is also a factor in itself. On the one hand, term limits and a radically changed political balance in most statehouses mean that few sitting legislators or board members remember the relatively sophisticated debates about the merits and demerits of standardized testing that took place a decade ago. Unacquainted with alternatives, most such legislators naively see tests as promising and uncomplicated policy tools—just as their predecessors initially did. More ominously, many governing boards are now populated by a new cast of characters—actively political and quite explicit in their desire to dictate what is taught in public colleges and universities. SUNY's interest in standardized testing, for instance, is part of a wider pattern of proactive involvement in curricular matters designed to reverse what many board members feel has been a dangerous erosion of academic standards. Holding campuses accountable for educational results through testing is seen as one of many steps—including required core courses and incentive budgeting approaches—that will both increase system productivity and ensure that students are being taught what they should know.

These reasons for interest in standardized testing raise some intriguing issues, however. One somewhat surprising development is that this new wave of testing proposals has so far encountered neither righteous nor reasoned resistance from the academy. Both reactions, of course, were characteristic of prior attempts to enact such measures. At SUNY, to be sure, faculty union representatives raised the usual objections to testing before the board in the spring, but grassroots opposition seemed lackluster in comparison to what happened in New Jersey and Washington years ago. In Utah, few at the universities (at least as of this writing) appear either threatened or excited by the initiative. Part of the reason in both cases may be a growing ho-hum attitude toward accountability in general that's the product of more than fifteen years of sustained government pressure: many academic leaders may have come to believe that, as with taxes and pollution, nothing can be done except to live with it.

At the same time, the essentially conservative educational and political philosophy that undergirds current initiatives contains real dilemmas about how a testing program ought to be organized. On the one hand, the creation of national K–12 standards, backed by assessment, is exactly the agenda now being advanced by the Clinton White House— and being vehemently opposed by conservative leaders on the grounds of state and local rights. Indicative here is the fact that contemporary Republican-led fiscal proposals in New York that would create clear winners and losers among SUNY institutions are already being actively opposed by equally conservative legislators whose own campuses might be adversely affected. More important, the academic content being advocated by the New Right as the foundation of reinvigorated standards is not what available standardized instruments test. Rooted in the assessment demands of the eighties, examinations like the COMP, the CAAP, the C-BASE, and the Academic Profile focus far more on crosscutting academic skills such as communication and critical thinking than on knowing the traditional canons of literature, science, and Western civilization. Building new tests will cost money, however—exactly what efficiency-minded board members want to avoid.

Meanwhile, the realities of implementing large-scale testing programs in college and university settings remain as intractable as ever. Both Utah and SUNY—like Arkansas and Wisconsin—seem unwilling so far to make test performance a condition for student advancement. Problems of motivation under such conditions have been apparent from the beginning and will probably continue to be encountered in such programs. Similarly, both states' proposals recommend testing samples of students rather than full populations. Again, experience elsewhere suggests that once a state is committed to such a program, all affected students will have to be tested, if only on grounds of equity and logistical convenience. Again, these practical problems lead to higher costs, and sustained attention and unbroken political will will be required to overcome them.

Neither of these intangibles is in great supply in the states these days. As is also the case with complex performance funding schemes, statewide testing proposals may prove immensely popular among policymakers yet be impossible to implement because sufficient long-term consensus cannot be forged to make them work. Equally relevant is the fact that the conservative standards revolution that lies behind recent testing proposals is really directed toward what is taught and how, not toward how much is learned. If sufficient political capital is mustered to sustain a change effort, it will likely be directed more toward the heart of the curriculum than toward launching a complex and costly testing program.

Whatever the outcome, the latest round of statewide testing proposals is disturbing, if only because we have been through all this before. Like most summer remakes, though, we can probably count on statewide testing's sequel this year to be much like its fellows in the movie industry: cheaper, shorter, and a good deal less subtle and sophisticated than the original.

Performance Indicators and Performance Funding (1989–2000)

In 1989–1990, the boom in state-mandated assessment was attenuated by a recession, which shifted state interest in performance and limited the resources they had available to support assessment. No new mandates were enacted and, while many remained officially on the books, staff cutbacks meant that they were not really enforced. At the same time, more pointed state interest in efficiency and productivity meant that evaluative attention turned markedly toward performance indicators for public institutions. Unlike the trend in assessing learning up to this point, which had largely avoided direct comparisons of institutions, the kinds of statistical performance measures chosen—cost per credit, graduation rates, and faculty productivity—centered on publicly-reported tables of comparative information.

Meanwhile, state interest in incenting public colleges and universities toward higher performance led to a spike of interest in pay-for-performance. Where Tennessee was once the sole example of performance funding, about a third of the states had instituted a performance funding program by 1995. For a variety of reasons including political backlash from institutions, funding shortfalls, and the sheer complexity of managing such programs, most were gone by the end of the decade. The seven columns in this section describe these developments in the 1990s.

Performance Indicators:
A New Round of Accountability

From Assessment Update 5:3 (1993).

Many have noted that state higher education policy agendas have now tilted strongly toward accountability, with marked impacts on state approaches to assessment. Another manifestation of this shift in many states, though less openly discussed, is the rapid development of statistical performance indicators as a quick answer to higher education's accountability "problem." In the last three months, under the auspices of an Education Commission of the States project aimed at charting and analyzing these developments, I've had an occasion to look at what's happening in ten states and to make some preliminary generalizations. In my column this issue I'd like to look briefly at the broader context for the development of state performance indicators, to examine some themes of implementation, and to describe specifically what these schemes require.

One place to start is by asking how the current accountability conversation resembles the one that launched assessment some seven years ago. One major difference in accountability's "new look" is its considerably wider domain. While the emergence of state interest in assessment in the mid-eighties signaled a concern with "quality" in opposition to more traditional elements, such as access and efficiency, current requirements demand both. Partly this is a matter of changing context. Most states initially approached assessment in good (or at best, fiscally neutral) times, and could afford to consider "quality" as an add-on. Now, states recognize, hard times require doing more with less: gaining "quality" without sacrificing efficiency and access. As a result, the current crop of indicators proposals mixes new and old elements. Most appear dominated by a concern with traditionally defined efficiency, but many—like South Carolina's new requirement to report such things as the number of undergraduate students actively participating in sponsored-research activities—reflect a new concern with explicit educational processes and delivery as well.

One way that the move toward indicators looks like early state efforts in assessment, though, is in the incredible speed of its evolution. Kentucky's SB 109, South Carolina's Act 225, and New Mexico's "report card bill" look alike because their architects directly and rapidly informed one another in a pattern that might truly be labeled "legislation by fax." Indicators proposals in other states arose in very different ways (Wisconsin's, for instance, was an indirect product of a "blue ribbon" task force on faculty compensation!), but because of both a small body of available state-level data and limited technical possibilities for manipulating it, these proposals have ended up with a good deal in common. Most emerging indicators systems, for example, contain in total some 15 to 20 distinct data items collected by the state higher education governing or coordinating body and are reported in the form of direct comparisons among institutions or sectors. In contrast to state assessment initiatives, moreover, the majority of new indicators schemes have a visible connection to funding. Though only a few states (Texas and Arkansas, for instance) appear to be joining Tennessee in an explicitly performance-based approach, many (like South Carolina or New York) do link reporting compliance with base funds eligibility or access to a variety of special purpose funds. Also in contrast to most early assessment initiatives, state authorities have been less willing to change proposed requirements when faced with initial (and often vociferous) protests from institutions. The predominant attitude has been hard line: that higher education has up to now "escaped" the kinds of real accountability measures applied to other state agencies and that this situation is no longer tolerable.

What, finally, are these states collecting indicators about? Probably the most common single item is graduation/retention rates, often compiled via existing state-level unit record systems. A second frequently included component is graduate placement, either in field-related employment or in further postsecondary education. Somewhat similar are requirements to provide "linkage" data across educational sectors such as community college to four-year transfer rates, or reports directed toward primary feeder high schools. Reflecting concerns with instructional quality, a third category of indicators directly examines instructional practices; several states, for instance, require institutions to report the proportion of lower-division credits delivered by full-time faculty. Finally, some indicators lists do indeed contain cognitive outcomes, though most states have continued to avoid proposals for expensive common testing. Wisconsin's, for example, contains a proposal for end-of-sophomore-year testing using the ACT-CAAP, while a number of SREB states are engaged in exploratory conversations with ETS about administering a version of New Jersey's task-based General Intellectual Skills test discontinued by that state some two years ago.

These preliminary findings signal a return of legislative interest in simple "bottom-line" answers about higher education's performance. With times as tough as they are, these questions will be much harder for us to duck than in their first "assessment-mandate" incarnation. Now, as then, we'd best be ready with workable alternatives.

Performance Funding: New Variations on a Theme

From Assessment Update 6:4 *(1994).*

The idea of performance funding has intrigued state leaders for more than a decade, but until recently Tennessee remained its solitary example. As state "indicators" systems have proliferated, however—and as higher education's accountability problem has become more urgent—more states have started to move in this direction. Texas had a significant encounter with the concept last year, but largely because of its high-stakes nature this initiative remains on indefinite hold. Arkansas, Kentucky, and Missouri have proceeded less spectacularly and more deliberately.

Missouri's initiative, now three years old, provides a case in point. Titled "Funding for Results" (FFR), its origins date from 1989, when this state began reexamining its "base plus" approach to public university funding and looking for a means to encourage quality improvement. As in Tennessee more than fifteen years before, state higher education leaders in Missouri were searching for new ways to "sell" higher education to legislators facing flat revenues and escalating alternative priorities for expenditure. Also as in Tennessee, FFR came out of the state's Coordinating Board for Higher Education (CBHE), which worked in consultation with the institutions themselves. Partly because of these factors, an FFR component has been successfully a part of Missouri's plan for providing funding allocations to public four-year institutions since 1991—beginning with a .5% set-aside to fund the program, with a planned increase to 2% to 3%. Last year, this approach (both base-plus and FFR) was extended to the state's two-year colleges, whose previous state allocations were based entirely on a growth-oriented cost-per-credit-hour reimbursement formula.

Proceeding slowly, Missouri was able to learn from previous state-level performance funding initiatives and to keep up with more recent developments. In contrast to Tennessee, where outcomes measures in the form of the ACT-COMP examination and major field test results were included as performance criteria almost from the beginning, the Missouri initiative began with relatively noncontroversial and readily available statistics, including degrees awarded in identified "critical" fields and to minority students and, for two-year colleges, the number of students completing associate-degree requirements or transferring to senior institutions. Only last year were outcomes measures added to FFR: for example, the percentage of students scoring above the 50th percentile on nationally normed examinations. Even these were measures already required of institutions as part of the state's five-year-old assessment initiative implemented by executive order.

The architects of FFR chose not to embed performance parameters in complex statistical formulas. Most have instead been operationalized in terms of specified additional payments to institutions in return for each "unit" of desired activity. The 1995 fiscal year allocations, for instance, award a $1,000 bonus to four-year institutions for each baccalaureate degree granted to a minority student. This renders the approach easily understandable to both institutions and the lay public. Finally, marginal dollars allocated through FFR have been kept within manageable limits; current guidelines call for FFR to be between 2% and 3% of total instructional budget, well below Tennessee's current 5.5% or Texas's politically unsuccessful 10% marginal funding proposal.

While effective in launching FFR, these features did not really break new ground. But innovation is clearly apparent in CBHE's most recent intent to add a component that enables individual institutions to set their own performance targets and to be rewarded with additional funds for attaining them. The resulting two-tiered FFR proposal, still in the discussion stage at this writing, is designed to overcome difficulties that have up to now bedeviled performance funding approaches. One is how to handle differences among institutions with respect to mission and student clientele without "homogenizing" performance. While retaining a component based on common state-level measures, the additional tier of FFR potentially allows institutions to be rewarded for achieving mission-specific goals. A second advantage of the approach is its potential to increase institutional involvement and ownership. By providing incentives for colleges and universities to attain targets that they themselves establish, the process encourages priority setting in the first place. At the same time, it potentially avoids a major drawback of pure performance funding, namely, that only already-strong programs and institutions are rewarded even though the real imperatives for improvement may be elsewhere.

If implemented, this new look in performance funding may affect assessment practice considerably. Like the mandates of the 1980s, it encourages the development of locally owned measures and approaches. Institutions will be unable to qualify for "tier two" funding unless they can operationalize and measure what they hope to achieve. But unlike previous mandates that often isolate assessment as "a train on its own track," the approach promises to link institutional assessment with budgeting and planning from the outset. For this reason alone, FFR's proposed second tier looks like a program to watch.

————————

Putting It All on the Line: South Carolina's Performance Funding Initiative

From Assessment Update *9:1 (1997).*

When it comes to mandating accountability for higher education, South Carolina's legislature has pretty much led the pack. When institutional effectiveness provisions were written into legislation on broad-based education reform passed in 1988 ("the cutting edge"), South Carolina joined a handful of states requiring all public institutions to engage in assessment. With Act 255 in 1992, the state was also one of the first to go the next step—requiring comparative performance measures for public colleges and universities in report card format. Last spring, the legislature was at it again, passing Act 359, which requires that 100% of all state funding for higher education be allocated to colleges and universities on the basis of formally established performance measures.

In addition to refining mission areas for public institutions, Act 359 specifically delineates some 37 performance measures that are intended to replace the state's enrollment-driven funding formula by June 1999. Grouped under nine subheadings, the list itself contains few surprises. Prominent within it are such items as graduation rates, the accreditation status of accreditable programs, faculty workload measures, and measures of general efficiency (especially in administrative operations) —all of which have figured prominently in the performance measure initiatives of other states. But also apparent are interesting attempts to influence institutional good practice, an intent signaled earlier in South Carolina by Act 255's inclusion of "numbers of undergraduates participating in faculty research" as one of eleven report card indicators. Act 359 expands this category by including such domains as posttenure review, the availability of faculty to students outside the classroom, use of technology, and collaboration and cooperation across institutions and with the private sector. Such matters delve deeply into the ways institutions do business. At the same time, they are unusually resistant to the development of simple statistical measures.

Since July 1996, a steering committee and three task forces have been working under the auspices of the state's Commission on Higher Education to meet a January 1997 submission deadline for an implementation plan. By October, this effort had yielded relatively detailed operational definitions for each mandated measure, and, at present, sectoral committees are considering specific performance benchmarks and weights to drive an allocation formula. This represents an enormous achievement in a very short period of time (tight timelines are also characteristic of South Carolina's approach to accountability mandates), but the effort also has led the state in interesting directions.

First, it is not surprising that a lot of previous work on developing measures of institutional effectiveness has been incorporated wholesale. Much of this, of course, came from Act 255 and a good deal of it from the Southern Association of Colleges and Schools (SACS) and the Southern Regional Education Board (SREB) as well. Measures of faculty qualifications, for instance, draw heavily on established SACS criteria, which are far more explicit on this matter than those of other regional accreditation agencies. Measures of faculty compensation and institutional spending patterns, in turn, heavily reference benchmarks for peer states already established by the SREB. Workable approaches drawn from more unlikely sources are also being dusted off; in both job placement and graduation rate discussions, for example, traces are visible of the commission's substantial prior investment in developing outcomes measures for the State Postsecondary Review Entity. At least as important, South Carolina's long-term commitment to fostering an assessment infrastructure is paying off. Institutional assessment practitioners—through the South Carolina Higher Education Association Network originally established with state support in 1988 to develop institutional effectiveness guidelines—are reluctantly but prominently involved in the effort to design a workable system.

Despite these advantages, the task remains daunting. Although at least seven states now have performance funding schemes in place that incorporate outcomes to some degree, all rely on marginal incentives amounting to no more than about 5% of institutional allocations. Two previous attempts to base all state support on performance measures— one in Florida last year and another in Texas two years ago—were tabled as politically unworkable (though both remain formally in place). It is therefore not surprising that practitioners in South Carolina are trying hard to limit the system's scope. One such attempt was a proposal to put most of the weight in the performance formula on its mission focus criteria—essentially, whether the institution has a mission statement consistent with state guidelines and a program array to match. If successful, this approach would have effectively constrained the amount of money affected by harder performance criteria to about 10% to 15%. Although this initiative was quickly ruled out of order by the commission, more recent findings suggest, at least for the moment, that the state will follow the more traditional model of establishing a separate (though substantial) "performance pot" of resources to be allocated in addition to base.

Adding to the challenge is the fact that 37 indicators are a lot. Ironically, this could add a measure of built-in stability, if only because statistical fluctuations in a large number of equally low weighted dimensions will likely buffer any large changes in the bottom line. More seriously, many of the proposed performance criteria overlap in scope, and some are clearly more measurable than others. Mission focus measures, for instance, begin with relatively straightforward examinations of program structure, but they also raise questions about cost-effectiveness and goal achievement that are covered later by other, much better-conceived, measures. While a short-term solution to this problem has been found by allowing sectors to zero-weight redundant subdimensions to remove them from the formula, technical amendments may eventually be needed to clean up the system.

South Carolina's experience illustrates the difficulty of writing performance measures directly into law—a problem avoided by more mature applications of the performance funding concept in states like Tennessee and Missouri. At the same time, the many measures intended to tap institutional good practice remain essentially judgment calls. The proposed indicator on posttenure review of faculty, for in-stance, tests the institution's adherence to a set of a dozen best-prac-tice criteria for such processes, which will require somebody to review each institution's practices against this list to determine performance. Who will do this job and how they will behave when they know that such judgments will actually move money around remain to be seen. Again, prior experience in such states as Tennessee is instructive: Over time, allocation criteria have tended to rely more and more on hard (and increasingly refined) statistical measures in an attempt to head off charges of bias and to remove the inevitable political bargaining associated with judgment-based measures.

Whatever its eventual shape, South Carolina's program is probably a portent of things to come. Act 255 was widely imitated by legisla-tures in the early 1990s as states rushed to adopt report card measures, and at least six states have performance funding initiatives on the table for spring 1997. Similarly, Act 359 illustrates virtually every policy and technical dilemma associated with such an initiative. So whatever the outcome, other states will have something to learn. For both reasons, the South Carolina case will be a fruitful one to watch in the coming year.

Implementing Performance Funding in Washington State: Some New Takes on an Old Problem

From Assessment Update *10:3 (1998).*

Half a decade has gone by since states began joining Tennessee in using performance measures to allocate some portion of their public higher edu-cation dollars. Kentucky, Arkansas, and Missouri were among the first to do so. Now about ten states run formal performance funding programs, and a dozen more are seriously considering their adoption. Although for many this trend is worrisome, the emerging "second wave" of performance funding initiatives is a good deal more sophisticated than the last. Among the most interesting is under way in the state of Washington.

The political appeal of pay for performance remains undiminished. Indeed, enthusiasm for it has thus far spawned three attempts to allocate *all* public dollars to colleges and universities on this basis—two patently unsuccessful (in Texas and Florida) and one still under way (in South Carolina). But less extreme approaches have also proven difficult to implement. Once in place, moreover, it is hard to make them stick. At least one early adopter (Arkansas) is now out of business; as of this writing, it will likely be joined by another (Kentucky). For the most part, these difficulties are a product of sheer political instability. Implementing a successful performance funding policy—as Tennessee's fifteen-year experience graphically demonstrates—is a long-term business and is rarely gotten right the first time. But in many states these days, policymakers either cannot agree on the common goals needed to drive a performance funding program in the first place or cannot maintain consensus long enough to resist fatal meddling after a program is established.

Recent experience in Washington nicely illustrates many of the policy dilemmas involved. The state's approach also contains both innovative and problematic features that are present in other "second wave" performance funding states. The story begins with the Washington legislature's decision in 1997 to include a performance component for higher education in the state's 1996–1998 biennial budget (ESHB 2259, Sections 601 and 619). Governor Gary Locke was an active proponent of this initiative. Earlier, as a state legislator, Locke had been a visible supporter of the state's approach to assessment. What happened in assessment, in fact, helps explain what happened in performance funding—largely because of the policy tone that the earlier initiative established.

In 1989, Washington institutions successfully resisted a mandate by the Higher Education Coordinating Board (HECB) for a commonly administered sophomore test, substituting instead a policy based on local, institutionally developed measures. More significant, the legislature generously supported this more decentralized initiative through appropriations to individual colleges and universities. As a result, Washington is still one of the few places where mandated assessment activities are supported by state funds. Issues raised by assessment—institutional autonomy, the use of categorical funding to induce institutional action, and the policy roles of intermediate bodies like the HECB and the State Board for Community and Technical Colleges (SBCTC)—would all be revisited in acting out performance funding.

One important difference between Washington's approach and those of other states is that it was decentralized from the outset. In fact, the state has not one but two performance funding initiatives. For the six four-year institutions, the set-aside pot was designated to be 2% of the noninstructional budget, but because each institution is independently governed, incentive dollars were separately appropriated for each. To allocate these funds, five performance measures were established by law: (1) undergraduate student retention rates, (2) five-year graduation rates, (3) performance on a "graduation efficiency index" based on the ratio of actual credits completed and the number officially required for program completion, (4) a faculty productivity measure uniquely defined by each institution, and (5) an additional uniquely determined measure reflecting "mission attainment" for each institution. The HECB was charged with establishing rules for determining how much each institution could claim of "its" performance dollars, but was not itself given the money.

As a recognized governing body, though, the SBCTC was given both the money and the authority to allocate it directly to the state's 32 two-year institutions. From the outset, the SBCTC was thus able to adopt a more flexible approach, taking into account appropriate differences between institutions. In this case, the performance pot was established at 1% of total appropriations for the system as a whole. To allocate these dollars, explicit performance targets were set for four statewide outcomes: (1) the hourly wage of job-training program graduates, (2) the transfer rate of academic-track students to four-year institutions, (3) completion rates in core courses such as English and math, and (4) performance on the same "graduation efficiency index" used by the four-year institutions.

Both initiatives, though, involved taking money off the top—a strong break with established Washington tradition, as well as with the experiences of most other states using performance funding. One way or another, most of the latter have managed to create new money to support their ventures (or at least to create the appearance of doing so by establishing a visibly separate source of funds). Washington's experience confirms that the initial tone set by such moves is important. A more creative initial funding approach might have avoided the strong opposition to the measure by campus leaders, especially in the four-year sector, where the signal sent by the legislature implied restricting money that had already been appropriated.

Despite this drawback, both the SBCTC and the HECB have in part been able to adopt approaches that buffer the "hard linkages" between statistical performance levels and dollar amounts that are typical of other performance funding schemes. Hard linkages have always presented two fundamental problems. One is the lag effect inherent in almost all performance measures. Even if an institution takes immediate action to address a particular outcome (for example, a graduation or retention rate), it may be years before these actions pay off. Meanwhile, the institution continues to be penalized in an outcome-based performance scheme.

To address this difficulty, both the HECB and the SBCTC in Washington awarded performance funds for the first year of the biennium solely on the basis of institutional planning efforts aimed explicitly at improving performance on the statewide outcome measures. Going further, the SBCTC approach also required each two-year college to adopt a set of additional action or process measures, chosen from a statewide menu, that were expected to contribute to collective performance on these outcomes. Institutional fulfillment of locally established targets for these action measures would then be used by the board to help allocate performance dollars in the second year of the biennium.

The second historic problem with the use of hard linkages in performance funding is how to take into account factors outside an institution's control. Graduation and retention rates, for instance, are determined far more by incoming student ability levels than by anything that an institution can do. Institutions also may simply be unable to benefit from particular performance "opportunities" because of where they are and what they do—a difficulty apparent, for example, in Missouri's Funding for Results (FFR) program that rewards institutions explicitly for producing minority graduates. Two useful ways to address this problem are to focus principally on institutional improvement and to negotiate with institutions to establish individualized (and appropriately different) expectations. Both have been partially adopted by the HECB and the SBCTC. In the latter case, the board works directly with institutions to set appropriate targets for attaining statewide performance values, taking individual differences in context and capacity into account. In the four-year case, this approach is less feasible because *all* institutions are expected to attain the same statewide performance targets by 2005. There is some flexibility even here, however, because different performance increments have been negotiated for each institution for each intervening year.

A final promising feature of both Washington initiatives—pioneered by Missouri's FFR program several years ago—is their use of additional institution-specific measures that can be tailored to particular missions and contexts. As noted, the four-year program includes two institutionally defined measures in the group of five established in law. The SBCTC, in turn, requires each institution to identify an individualized set of process measures for which to be held accountable in the biennium's second year. The board may also allow colleges to set their own priorities regarding which of the four legislative outcomes measures they want to emphasize (and be rewarded for) in their local improvement plans.

On balance, the notion of establishing a few broad performance goals and allowing established governing or coordinating bodies the flexibility to allocate resources to institutions at different levels and in different ways to attain these targets as a *system*, seems a promising innovation for performance funding. So far, Washington's approach has come closest to testing this notion in practice. Colorado may adopt a similar approach next year. And although South Carolina's far more ambitious performance funding adventure will continue to grab most of the headlines, we may eventually learn just as much from the opposite corner of the country.

Accountability with a Vengeance: New Mandates in Colorado

From Assessment Update *12:5 (2000).*

Relations between legislatures and public colleges and universities are wary in any state. But over the years in Colorado, they have been especially rancorous and intimately bound up with assessment. As early as 1986, the state's General Assembly mandated assessment as part of House Bill 1187—one of the first to do so. It was a sign of things to come that this original legislation stipulated that institutions could lose up to 2% of their funding if they did not comply. The potentially harsh effects of HB1187 were mitigated in part by the Colorado Commission on Higher Education's (CCHE) implementation of it as an institution-centered initiative. This early action illustrated the buffering role that the CCHE was to play for some time as additional waves of accountability-related legislation were passed by the General Assembly, a role that often frustrated legislators who perceived the agency as getting in the way. With a gubernatorial turnover last year, though, the commission's role has changed. Sitting as the CCHE's chief executive is none other than the former chair of the assembly's powerful Joint Budget Committee and the architect of many of its most prescriptive provisions.

Roots of the current situation in Colorado can be traced back to 1996, when the legislature passed the first in a series of "new look" accountability initiatives (HB96-1219). Like its counterparts in many other states, this bill called for the establishment of a comprehensive,

comparative quality indicator system (QIS) for Colorado public institutions, which could eventually be linked to funding. Almost before its
provisions could be fielded, the assembly acted again by passing Sen-
ate Bill 99-229. This legislation amended HB96-1219's provisions to
include new outcomes measures, and it required explicit benchmarks
of performance to be established for all previously established quality
indicators. More significantly, Item XI-B of the new legislation called
for an assessment at graduation for all students, using, if possible, nationally normed standardized examinations. Item XI-C, in turn, required the
"assessment of competency in functional skills and basic literacy" for
all students at the end of the sophomore year. For Colorado, at least,
these features signaled an important change in the philosophy of student
outcomes assessment as a tool of state policy. While HB1187 had established the primary purpose of assessment as program evaluation intended
primarily to provide information about performance for purposes of public communication and improvement, SB99-229, as in states like Florida
and Texas, is designed to provide gatekeeping for individual students
as well. In pursuit of this policy goal and with support from the CCHE,
six Colorado institutions are currently pilot-testing the ETS Academic
Profile, although it is an odd choice of instrument for this purpose. By
2001–2002, the CCHE plans to use the results of both the sophomore
and the graduation assessments in performance funding.

Other prominent ingredients of the new Colorado initiative high-
light two long-standing legislative concerns: faculty productivity and
administrative overhead costs. With regard to the former, the CCHE's
approach to implementation is both clever and prescriptive. The measure adopted in essence establishes a "typical" faculty work week based
on "teaching-related" hours, using the methodology incorporated in
the federally conducted National Survey of Postsecondary Faculty. But
rather than benchmarking each institution's performance against these
established national standards, as might then be expected, the CCHE
chose to establish benchmarks within each institutional sector, based
on the results achieved by its highest-performing member. An identical procedure was used to benchmark administrative overhead costs

and several other performance measures, even in cases where national data are available. The logic here is compellingly disingenuous: the fact that somebody achieved this level of performance demonstrates that it is possible, so why not expect it of everybody? This method, of course, pits institutions directly against one another in competition—a feature avoided up to now by most state-level performance funding schemes, which establish benchmarks so that all institutions can potentially win. More subtly, Colorado's approach allows statistical outliers to drive the entire calculation. Many of the "faculty teaching-related work week" numbers used in implementation discussions on benchmarking between the CCHE and the institutions this spring, for example, substantially exceed the average work week expected of a Colorado civil servant! Such outcomes might at first glance suggest naivete, but state actors knew exactly what they were doing. Getting tenure-track faculty at the University of Colorado to teach more hours—especially at its flagship Boulder campus—has been at the top of many a legislator's "to do" list for many years, and exactly how logically this objective is accomplished is of relatively little importance in the current political climate.

All told, the quality indicator system currently contains 29 discrete items—not so many as South Carolina's recently implemented performance funding scheme, to be sure (37), but a lot to define and keep track of. Many of the indicators mirror the kinds of measures adopted by other states, including graduation rates, pass rates on licensure examinations, GPAs of transfer students, and student satisfaction surveys. But others, like the faculty workload measures described above, reflect some very specific and long-standing legislative concerns. For instance, two indicators concentrate on the availability of required and core course sections at each campus. Their presence in the list stems from a prominent theory among legislators that the principal reason for the long times to graduation (defined as anything more than four years) typical of Colorado students is faculty unwillingness to offer sufficient sections of courses students needed to graduate. Like many other items in the QIS, moreover, these measures read more like stipulations than indicators, prescribing specific ratios of sections to be offered for particular numbers of freshmen enrolled. Similarly constructed items address the faculty teaching role more specifically. Three indicators, for example, require regular faculty teaching evaluations, mandatory attendance at professional development activities to improve teaching for those found wanting, and identifiable implications for the improvement of teaching and learning present in at least half of all unsponsored faculty research activities. Both sets of measures, though they nominally apply to all institutions, appear to be directed at the state's flagship campus—the only place where complaints on such topics as course availability and faculty inattention to teaching have actually surfaced. Finally, like many of South Carolina's performance funding indicators, a substantial number of the items in Colorado's QIS are not measures at all. Instead, they consist of a range of "yes/no" stipulations that will be attested to by the institution's president and subject to audit by CCHE. Among the topics so addressed are implementing and evaluating a student advising system consistent with guidelines established by the Colorado Student Association and taking specific actions to cooperate with the state's K–12 system as prescribed in other legislation.

By any account, this is a formidable list, and despite the now close political alignment between the CCHE and the legislature, its very complexity raises doubts about feasibility. At the same time, wider features of the Colorado political landscape make implementing *anything* difficult. Performance funding and mandated student assessment, for instance, are both hampered by the state's byzantine governance structure for higher education: six separate governing boards with independent authority, each of which controls one or more institutions. In the realm of performance funding, this means that the CCHE must allocate performance-based dollars to boards, not to individual institutions—although the amounts available for allocation are based on institution-level performance. In the realm of assessment, in turn, only the boards have the authority to set graduation requirements for the institutions they govern; this means that the choice of what actually constitutes a "graduation year assessment" for academic programs will in each case be up to them.

Nor does the legislature appear ready to appropriate substantial new dollars to support performance funding. Indeed, as in many states that have recently adopted such systems, the entire scheme applies only to new money. The result this year—the first in which performance funding was tried using the QIS—was that 9 of the 29 indicators were used, with considerable controversy and trouble, to allocate what seemed to be very small amounts of money for most participants.

These difficulties illustrate some wider trends now apparent in state accountability policy. One is a new aggressiveness in many states, often promoted by a more politicized state higher education agency. Almost a dozen states now resemble Colorado in having an ex-legislator or other political figure as SHEEO. Such leadership often means the establishment of more narrowly prescriptive measures focused, as in Colorado, on such matters as curriculum and faculty productivity. These actors are also much more likely than their predecessors to adopt an outcomes agenda founded on standardized testing, which based on previous K–12 experience they find both reassuringly familiar and appropriately "tough." But the Colorado experience is also proving typical because it is sufficiently ambitious and complicated to raise real doubts about practicability. Both performance funding and mandated statewide testing are agendas that require considerable time to unfold, that demand unbroken agency attention to countless implementation details to be successful, and that will be resisted by institutions at every turn. In the case of performance funding, these challenges have meant that almost as many states have abandoned the approach as have adopted it over the past few years. In the case of statewide testing, state initiatives that only a year ago had strong momentum (as in Utah and SUNY) now appear on hold. Only time will tell if Colorado's attempt to implement both simultaneously will ultimately be successful in the face of these precedents and challenges. What seems certain in the short term, though, is that public colleges and universities in Colorado are in for a rough time.

Smoke Signals from the Hills of Texas

From Assessment Update 18:3 (2006).

Since the emergence of assessment as an element of state policy in the mid-1980s, state leaders have always looked first to their K–12 systems for examples of how to proceed. As a result, college and university leaders have worried that the sweeping, heavily assessment-based elementary and secondary school reforms embodied in the No Child Left Behind (NCLB) legislation enacted in 2002 would spill over into higher education. Less noticed until recently was the Texas connection. NCLB was based in large part on similar legislation that had been enacted earlier in Texas, and the "Texas miracle" that claimed considerable gains for schoolchildren on standardized achievement tests—as well as significant narrowing of achievement gaps between white and minority students—was cited extensively in the process of enacting the national measure. The U.S. secretary of education, Margaret Spellings, is from Texas and was prominent in implementing the Texas program, as was her predecessor Rod Paige.

It should be no surprise, therefore, that much of the early discussion about higher education accountability emanating from the Secretary of Education's Commission on the Future of Higher Education has been similarly informed by a Texas connection. The chairman of the commission, Charles Miller, a strong advocate of test-based accountability, oversaw the development of a comprehensive accountability approach for the University of Texas (UT) system when he was head of its board of regents. Miller has invited extensive testimony on what UT has done and makes no secret of the fact that he believes that it points the way forward.

The UT accountability system that formed the centerpiece of discussion at the December meeting of the Spellings Commission was a long time in coming. Miller first proposed it to the UT regents in 1999, when he was heading UT's Academic Affairs Committee. The first incarnation was a campus-based assessment system, with each institution proposing and reporting on its own measures. When the regents' staff looked at the resulting draft reports, though, they had the same reaction that their counterparts had had ten years earlier when viewing similar materials for the State Council on Higher Education in Virginia: The assessment efforts of individual institutions were often of high quality, but they didn't add up to consistent systemwide accountability. When a new chancellor, Mark Yudof, arrived in the middle of 2002 amid growing political consensus on both the Texas school reforms and the emerging NCLB legislation, the regents became more proactive about common measures. The result was a charge to develop a new systemwide accountability framework.

This task was accomplished rapidly in consultation with the UT system's nine regular campuses and six health sciences centers. The basics of the framework were defined by the end of 2002, and enough measures were in place to provide an initial report to the legislature in March 2004. This rapid pace was prescient, because in January 2004, Governor Rick Perry issued Executive Order RP 31, which required the boards of all Texas public institutions to "direct that each institution and system work with the Higher Education Coordinating Board to develop a comprehensive system of accountability . . . [to provide] the information necessary to determine the effectiveness and quality of the education students receive at individual institutions." This order, in turn, was part of a wider governor's initiative involving similar executive orders directed at every state agency.

In its design and contents, the current UT accountability system is indeed comprehensive. It is organized around four areas of performance—(1) student access, success, and outcomes; (2) teaching, research, and health care excellence; (3) service to and collaboration with communities; and (4) organizational efficiency and productivity—with a fifth section devoted to individual institutional profiles and comparisons to help each institution set or revise goals. Its main section contains no fewer than seventy-two comparative indicators reported at the institutional level, many of which have been tracked over a five-year period in order to examine trends. Reminiscent of both the Texas school reforms and NCLB, a number of indicators focus on reducing performance gaps between white students and students of color. Moreover, following the current fashion in state policy, some measures are featured as targets in the individually tailored "institutional compacts" that are negotiated each year between the board and institutions.

Most of the measures in the UT framework—for example, graduation and persistence rates, the percentage of lower-division credits taught by tenure-track faculty, and space utilization ratios—are used by other states for similar purposes. But some of them—especially in the all-important realm of undergraduate quality—are new. Among the twenty indicators used to examine the quality of undergraduate education are pass rates for licensure examinations (in teaching, nursing, and engineering), comparative results on selected items drawn from the National Survey of Student Engagement (including satisfaction with advising, evaluation of the overall educational experience, and the percentage reporting that they would attend the same institution if they were starting over again), and comparative campus performance on the Collegiate Learning Assessment (CLA) offered by the Council on Aid to Education (CAE).

The CLA was administered in 2004–2005 to samples of 100 freshmen and 100 seniors at each of the nine UT undergraduate campuses, and a second cycle of testing is under way for 2005–2006. Results of the first administration were presented to the board last February as part of the second annual accountability report, using a scheme that is both ambitious and complex. Separate mean scores are first reported for each population for each campus on each of the two components of the assessment—(1) a performance task that requires students to demonstrate problem-solving and communication skills in response to a scenario-based situation and (2) a writing task based on the "make or break an argument" prompts used on the Graduate Record Examination. The system also reports on two benchmark measures—(1) the national "expected scores" on the CLA for freshmen and seniors and (2) a uniquely calculated "expected score" on the CLA for each population at each institution. Expected scores are a hallmark of CAE's approach to CLA reporting; they are intended to reveal the value added by education.

They consist of regression-based predictions of how students ought to perform on the assessment, given their entering SAT or ACT scores. In addition, the system reports a "difference score" that compares actual senior performances with the corresponding expected performances. On most of these comparisons, the accompanying text notes that UT campuses performed either "as expected" or "above expected" (although inspection of the actual numbers is less conclusive). It is notable that UT avoided the temptation of directly comparing freshman with senior performances, a comparison based on cross-sectional samples that would have been severely compromised by student attrition.

A second set of graphics plots actual performance ranges for the middle 50 percent of each institution's composite score distribution against its national equivalent. Separate plots are provided for freshmen and for seniors. These are clever displays on the face of it because they avoid the false precision of mean scores based on limited numbers of cases, as well as averting the challenge of trying to explain the complex logic behind expected versus actual scores. When presented this way, there appear to be very few meaningful differences between UT student performance and the national sample.

A third set of graphics reverts to the value-added construct by presenting the difference between each institution's actual and expected composite scores separately for freshmen and for seniors. The final display in this series tries to portray value added explicitly by plotting, in the words of the report, the "difference between seniors' scores relative to the national group, with the freshman scores relative to the national sample" (p. 57). UT institutions again look pretty good on these comparisons, but it may be hard for lay audiences to track what is actually portrayed here, because the underlying scores have by now been through a great many calculations.

The 2006 UT System Accountability Report (http://www.utsystem .edu/IPA/acctrpt/2005/completereport.pdf) is the second major publication featuring the use of CLA scores as part of a comparative performance metric. The first was *Measuring Up 2004*, which presented CLA results together with ten other state-level learning indicators for five states participating in a national demonstration project funded by The Pew Charitable Trusts (see Ewell, 2005). Like its predecessor, the UT report benchmarked CLA results against available national levels of performance and used the CLA as only one of an array of related measures. Similarly, the UT report used carefully crafted graphics to portray its underlying "story line" for lay policymakers, whose eyes glaze over when presented with columns of numbers. Finally, it seems clear that like the Measuring Up pilot, the UT testing initiative encountered familiar implementation difficulties in obtaining usable student CLA results, probably due to difficulties with student recruitment and motivation. For example, freshman scores are provided for only six of the nine UT campuses and senior scores for only seven because there were insufficient data for some campuses. Indeed, careful footnote readers of both reports will note the many caveats on the use of CLA results and strong warnings that not too much should be made of any given data point.

But there are also important differences between the UT report and the *Measuring Up* report. The Measuring Up pilot avoided results for individual institutions, both because its expressed purpose was to establish state-level benchmarks and because the sample sizes used (identical to those in the UT initiative) were deemed insufficient to treat the data any other way. More important, because the objective was to benchmark absolute achievement levels as a measure of statewide "educational capital," the Measuring Up pilot made no attempt to gauge value added. As a result, it was able to tell a far simpler story. In the last analysis, the principal impact of both reports was less about what the reported CLA results said about comparative performance and more about the political message sent by the fact of reporting them at all.

This thought leads us back to the Spellings Commission. Media interest in the CLA spiked in mid-February (following the lead of a *New York Times* article by Karen W. Arenson on February 9, 2006) because Chairman Miller made so much of the instrument and its potential for improved accountability. As of this writing, it is far from apparent whether the chairman will succeed in persuading his colleagues on the commission of the merits of this approach by the time they must report in August. But the message in the smoke signals from the hills of Texas is clear.

References

Arenson, K. W. (2006, Feb. 9). Panel Explores Standard Tests for Colleges. *New York Times*, p. A-1.

Ewell, P. T. (2005, September–October). Looking Back on "The Year of Accountability." *Assessment Update*, *17*(5), 9–11.

New Looks in Performance Measures: Indicator Systems in Two States

From Assessment Update *20:3 (2008).*

For states, the early 1990s were the halcyon days of performance measures. Within five years, more than two-thirds of the states had established comparative performance indicator systems for their public colleges and universities and results were presented publicly. For the most part, the statistics used were readily accessible and easy to count—things like graduation rates, instructional costs per student, or average admissions test scores. In many states, money was tied to measures in the form of performance funding. And virtually all of them yielded weighty accountability reports, issued annually or biennially, that presented long columns of numbers that few people ever looked at.

This rhythm of performance reporting was checked in many states by the recession at the turn of the century. No new money meant the end of performance funding in the states in which it had always been funded as an add-on. Complex indicator systems also required expensive staffs, so strapped SHEEO agencies increasingly abandoned them. But a new policy climate that emphasizes outcomes and societal return on investment is driving renewed interest in performance measures today. Two good examples of the new look in performance measurement are being rolled out this year by college and university systems in Minnesota and Washington.

The board of the Minnesota State College and University System (MnSCU) formally adopted the Board of Trustees Accountability System in November 2007. Two years in the making and consistent with MnSCU's strategic plan, the accountability system is built around ten core measures that display both institutional and system performance through dynamic Web-based graphics. The system was pilot-tested throughout the spring and formally adopted in March. Meanwhile, the State Board of Community and Technical Colleges (SBCTC) in Washington unveiled an initiative to measure institutional performance and to reward institutions for improving their levels of student achievement. Under this scheme, colleges can earn additional funding for improving their performance on outcome measures centered on student progress ranging from the completion of basic skills work to persistence in college and earning a credential. SBCTC's system was also some years in the making, and 2007–2008 is SBCTC's learning year for the new funding approach. Actual allocations based on performance will begin next year.

These two new approaches to constructing and using performance indicators are distinctive in several ways. First, they use some innovative measures. The MnSCU system, for instance, is built around ten indicators grouped under four main headings: access and opportunity, quality programs and services, meeting state and regional needs, and innovation and efficiency. As some of these labels suggest, the conceptual orientation of the system is as much about service to the state and its citizens as it is about the functioning of individual institutions. This is a trend that has become more and more apparent since publication of the first fifty-state report card on higher education, *Measuring Up*, in 2000. Also consistent with *Measuring Up*'s basic approach is the fact that statewide or system-level issues are addressed in both states. Implementing statewide measures effectively sometimes means using a different kind of measure at each level. In the MnSCU measures, for instance, a system-level indicator under access and opportunity is average tuition and fees in each collegiate sector as a percentage of median family income. But it makes little sense to report this indicator as an institutional performance measure because colleges have no control over the income levels of the students they are obligated to serve. Therefore, to hold individual institutions accountable for contributing to statewide performance on this indicator, the corresponding indicator at the institutional level is annual percentage increase in tuition and fees—something that institutions can actually control.

The conceptual orientation of MnSCU's system is as much about service to the state and its citizens as it is about the functioning of individual institutions.

The latest national thinking about accountability generated by the Spellings Commission is reflected in four of the ten indicators in the MnSCU system: high-quality learning, student engagement, partnerships, and innovation. Recognizing the fact that it is better to take the time needed to develop measures in meaningful areas of performance rather than just grab available numbers regardless of topic, MnSCU has elected to build these four measures later. High-quality learning will probably be measured by an advanced examination or a portfolio system, while student engagement will likely be measured by a student survey like the National Survey of Student Engagement.

SBCTC's performance funding scheme rests on a set of interrelated measures that are called *momentum points* because they describe milestones that mark student progress toward a credential or degree. A first set of momentum points evaluates college-level skills. Points are awarded for things like making significant gains in basic mathematics scores, number of students who have completed precollegiate coursework in basic skills, or number of students who have completed a GED. Another set of momentum points is awarded for things like number of students who complete fifteen and thirty college credits. Points in a third set are given for the number of students who complete core course requirements in writing or quantitative reasoning. A final set of points relates to the ultimate end of the student progression; for example, points can be earned for the number of students who earn a degree or certificate or the number who complete apprenticeship training. Development of these variables was informed by Washington community colleges' experience in the Achieving the Dream project funded by the Lumina Foundation for Education. The resulting measures represent a considerable advance over three-year associate degree completion rates for first-time full-time students (the measure traditionally used to measure community college performance) because they describe a far greater share of community colleges' student populations and are much more consistent with the missions of community colleges.

A second way in which the MnSCU and SBCTC initiatives are distinctive is that they rest upon sophisticated student unit record (SUR) databases. While many first-generation performance measures in the 1990s used SUR data, the elements tapped were limited to the kinds of data collected and archived at that time including items like term enrollments, credit hours, and degrees granted. Since then, state-level SUR systems have become steadily more sophisticated, and they are now able to support longitudinal student tracking across multiple institutions. Both MnSCU and SBCTC have SUR databases that contain transcript-level detail, enabling them to look at student success in far more detail than just term-to-term retention and completion. In SBCTC's case, additional data on noncredit offerings are available. Key outcomes like earning a GED or advancing to a higher level of literacy are not part of the credit system but are available to SBCTC researchers through noncredit records. The resulting student achievement database is a highly capable research tool, with applications far beyond supporting performance funding.

Third, the manner in which data are used and reported in these new initiatives demonstrates new thinking. For example, the MnSCU accountability system is a dashboard presented dynamically on the Web. Each of the ten core indicators is represented by a semicircular dial with a needle that registers the current level of performance. Zones around the radius of the dial are color coded red for "needs attention," blue for "meets expectations," and yellow for "exceeds expectations." Menu options provide greater levels of detail, historical trends, or quick links to explanations and definitions. Other Web pages behind the basic dashboard show the number of colleges in each performance category for each measure, provide a comparative look at selected groups of institutions, or display trend lines. The tricky bit of analysis that lies behind these dynamic displays is how to choose the cut points that delineate the various performance categories. Although a lot of historical data on the six established measures is already available to MnSCU staff, a major objective of the pilot is to determine how sensitive the dashboard is to data shortcomings or to relatively minor variations in performance.

Meanwhile, in the SBCTC scheme, the way data are used to drive funding decisions reflects much good thinking about how incentives can actually improve institutional performance. In contrast to most performance funding approaches in the mid-1990s, in which institutions were graded against system or peer averages, Washington community colleges will be benchmarked against themselves. Colleges are rewarded for each momentum point earned above the previous highest annual level of performance, and there is no upper limit to the number of points that can be earned by a college. If a college's enrollment declines, levels of expected performance are adjusted accordingly. Dollar levels allocated to the program are set conservatively so that all funds will be distributed in each cycle, and unawarded points can be banked for future funding. Funds awarded through momentum points become a permanent part of the base budget of each institution. Also unlike most previous state-level performance funding schemes, SBCTC's is very simple. Only a few measures of performance are used, their definitions are clear, and improvement over past performance is easy to demonstrate. Simplicity is also a deliberate feature of the MnSCU accountability approach, which uses only ten core measures.

In contrast to most performance funding approaches in the mid-1990s, in which institutions were graded against system or peer averages, Washington community colleges will be benchmarked against themselves. Washington community colleges are rewarded for each momentum point earned above the previous highest annual level of performance, and there is no upper limit to the number of points that can be earned by a college. Funds awarded through momentum points become a permanent part of the base budget of each institution.

Finally, both systems were developed on the basis of empirical research and the direct involvement of higher education scholars. SBCTC's momentum points scheme, for example, was the result of a research collaboration between the system's staff and researchers at the Community College Research Center at Teachers College, Columbia University. Moreover, while designing the performance funding component of the initiative, SBCTC interviewed scholars who had studied such mechanisms in other states to identify best practices. Similarly, MnSCU's accountability system incorporated extensive research on best practices obtained from other states and from scholars who study such practices.

Most of the visible action on higher education accountability in the last two years has occurred at the national level, driven by the Spellings Commission and the reauthorization of the Higher Education Act. The initiatives in Minnesota and Washington remind us that the states have been busy, too.

———————————

SECTION THREE

Beyond the States (2002–2009)

By about 2000, states were largely supplanted as the main external stimulus for assessment by regional accrediting organizations which, stimulated by new rulemaking by the federal Department of Education, were becoming considerably more aggressive in requiring institutions to engage in assessment. At the same time, the federal government itself increasingly became an accountability player—a process that culminated with the creation of the "Spellings Commission" in 2006. The four columns in this final section, all from the initial decade of the twenty-first century, detail these new developments in accreditation and the national accountability conversation.

Taking Stock of Accreditation Reform

From Assessment Update *14:1 (2002).*

Regional accreditation has largely surpassed state mandates as an initial reason for colleges and universities to engage in assessment. Stimulated in part by federal recognition policies, all six regional accrediting associations have moved visibly to incorporate greater attention to student learning in their standards. Most have also been actively reinventing their processes for reviewing institutions, rendering them more flexible, streamlined, and outcome-centered.

Behind much of this activity is a significant investment in accreditation reform on the part of The Pew Charitable Trusts. Through a grant package amounting to over $5 million, Pew funded four regional accrediting bodies—the North Central Association (NCA), the Southern Association of Colleges and Schools (SACS), the New England Association of Schools and Colleges (NEASC), and the Western Association of Schools and Colleges (WASC)—to undertake various projects aimed at changing current practices. The Pew package also includes support for two newly established accrediting bodies—the Teacher Education Accreditation Council (TEAC) and the American Academy of Liberal Education (AALE)—and underwrites two additional projects intended to develop new tools for presenting evidence and for conducting accreditation reviews. Last fall, Pew decided to take stock of its investment by conducting a systematic evaluation of accomplishments to date. What the evaluation found was both daunting and enlightening.

Pew's original interest in accreditation was stimulated by the potential for nongovernmental, peer-based accountability processes like accreditation to stimulate institutions and their faculties to take stronger collective responsibility for improving student learning—especially at the undergraduate level. The central premise underlying its grant-making was simple: if much of the current energy that accreditors devote to reviewing inputs and processes were redirected toward looking at outcomes, significant progress could be made toward improving student learning. Pew funding, moreover, was likely to enrich fertile ground, because several of the regional accreditors were already embarked on a broadly similar path of reform.

The resulting set of accreditation-related initiatives had many similar features, which included the following:

Streamlining the process. Many of these projects are trying to make the accreditation process less detailed and burdensome, and therefore more efficient. In some cases (for example, SACS and WASC), this means cutting the number of standards against which institutions are reviewed. In others (for example, AALE), it means developing quantitative indicators based on business practice, to speed review of such matters as fiscal condition and organizational sustainability. Greater efficiency, it is hoped, would allow more attention to be dedicated to examining teaching and learning.

Introducing greater flexibility. Responding to a common complaint that traditional accreditation did not add value to institutions, many of these projects also allow (or encourage) institutions to use accreditation to investigate topics of their own choosing. For instance, NCA's Academic Quality Improvement Project (AQIP), modeled on the Baldrige Award, concentrates almost entirely on the efforts of participating institutions to improve a selected number of internal practices. Again, it is hoped that at least some of these local topics will include student learning.

Promoting consistency. Several projects are attempting to make accreditation site visits more disciplined and consistent by adopting methods like the European academic audit process (which another Pew-funded effort researched and documented) and by employing rubric-based protocols for review. TEAC and AALE, for example, make extensive use of both; NCA's AQIP uses Baldrige-based protocols; and WASC is experimenting with several of these tools. These methods promote consistency in team judgments, but they are also intended to help pioneer new ways for review teams to approach the sticky issue of assessment.

Exploiting existing evidence. Rather than asking institutions to prepare extensive, specially prepared self-studies to ground a review, most of these projects emphasize assembling and documenting evidence more directly. Sometimes presentations of evidence take the form of a portfolio, a method also explored through a related Pew-funded effort— the Urban Universities Portfolio Project. In other cases, like TEAC's "inquiry brief" or the narratives associated with WASC's project and NCA's AQIP project, presentations are radically shortened and are more evidential than descriptive. Again, it is Pew's bet that much of the evidence discussed would be about student learning.

These are notable changes for a sometimes staid institution, and it is fair to say that Pew's support has had an impact. Institutions that have pioneered these new processes praise them for reduction of burden and the way they appear capable of simultaneously serving purposes of external accountability and internal improvement. But Pew's deeper look at its investment revealed some significant issues embedded in this approach to accreditation reform.

One is a basic change in the time-honored role of peer review. Since its beginnings, regional accreditation has relied on teams of individuals drawn from member institutions (and occasionally, but rarely, drawn from outside the region) to conduct institutional reviews. The underlying presumption here is one of mutual accountability and reliance on innate professional judgment. Except for an orientation to the region's standards, for example, most accrediting team members do not receive special training for the assignment. Indeed, they are encouraged to apply their own extensive experience as faculty members, administrators, student affairs professionals, librarians, and fiscal officers to observe and make judgments about what they find. The approaches adopted by Pew-funded projects, in contrast, can't be accomplished effectively by untrained reviewers. One reason for this is the fact that the new standards adopted by several of these agencies are no longer structured around visible and separable institutional resources and functions. WASC, for instance, replaced nine standards headed by traditional categories such as "faculty," "student services," "finance," and "academic programs" with four integrated performance-oriented standards with titles like "achieving educational objectives" and "creating an organization committed to learning and improvement." Standards structured in this manner can't just be divided among reviewers on the basis of individual expertise.

Another reason for improved training is the growing sophistication of review procedures themselves. Audit methods and the effective use of protocols to collect and examine evidence require familiarity and considerable practice to achieve consistent results. Because of this, TEAC and AALE reviewers undergo two days of intensive training before being sent into the field. Those participating in NCA's AQIP reviews, meanwhile, are trained through a process that parallels that of the industry-based Baldrige Award. WASC plans to develop training workshops of equivalent scope and complexity, centered on the nature of evidence and how to collect and appraise it on site. Further distancing some of these new processes from traditional peer review is the fact that TEAC's auditors are employees of the organization itself and that accreditors like WASC are considering formal certification of their trained reviewers.

Not surprisingly, the Pew evaluation noted shortfalls in reviewer training as one of the primary challenges to be faced as accreditors begin large-scale implementation of these new approaches. But the growing professionalization of the accreditation process that this entails also signals a notable shift away from the time-honored notion of peer review by colleagues who could count on a kind of informal academic connoisseurship to ground their quality judgments. This is a serious change, and its potential impacts have not been systematically examined.

Equally unsurprising is the fact that much of the need for greater training and discipline in review is driven by the growing emphasis on student learning embedded in these approaches. In light of accreditation's historic reliance on peer judgment, this is oddly ironic. When most regional accrediting bodies were founded, institutions were less diverse, so faculty peer reviewers could (at least in theory) be counted on to render consistent quality judgments about actual student performance— and it was not infrequent that they sampled student work directly. But such collective, albeit implicit, standards of acceptable college-level performance were one of the many casualties of our move toward a mass system of higher education in the 1960s and early 1970s. During this period, faculty retreated more and more into individual classrooms, where they currently remain sovereign. Meanwhile, they increasingly redirected any consequential peer-based judgments about quality toward research. In doing so, they lost both the ability and the inclination to make substantive and collective judgments about the overall quality of student performance.

This historical dynamic led in many ways toward accreditation's initial response to assessment, which began in the late 1980s and is still being played out today. The assessment of student learning was made an *additional* review requirement, implemented in the form of newly added standards such as "institutional effectiveness" in the case of agencies like

SACS and WASC or in the form of an additional assessment plan for NCA. Following the implicit process of division of labor that visiting teams had by then unconsciously adopted, the task of looking at institutions through this lens led inexorably to the appointment of designated assessment specialists, who were charged, like librarians and fiscal officers, with a particular review responsibility. Though the professional backgrounds of such team members were generally strong, the notion of peer-based judgment about real academic standards and actual levels of typical student performance in the classroom was further away than ever.

This is one of the most important conditions that the projects in the Pew accreditation portfolio are trying to address, and it is proving very hard to do. Underlying these projects is a shift in the underlying logic of external review from a model based on program evaluation toward a broader notion of academic quality assurance. The first is centered on demonstrating the effectiveness of learning outcomes directly and in the aggregate, using research-based methods to generate convincing evidence of average student attainment against institutionally determined goals. Such approaches usually employ methods that are consciously separated from the teaching and learning process in the name of objectivity. Academic quality assurance, in contrast, is centered on determining the degree to which meaningful standards of collective judgment are used in every instance in which faculty examine student performance. As one of the newly adopted WASC criteria for review puts it, "[the institution] demonstrates that its graduates consistently achieve stated levels of attainment and ensures that its expectations for student learning are embedded in the standards faculty use to evaluate student work." The difference is decisive for institutions, because the incentive provided by evaluation-based accreditation practice is to create organizationally visible assessment centers and programs *in addition to* regular processes of teaching and learning, while that associated with quality assurance-based assessment is to *transform* these processes themselves. Both require more sophisticated training and changes in review processes. But the second demands, in addition, a far more fundamental change in institutional culture.

Whether the majority of accreditors are ready for such a shift—or even realize that they are unconsciously moving toward it—is open to question. As the Pew evaluation pointed out, the amount of change that a voluntary association can impose on its members is ultimately determined by how much the members are willing to tolerate. No group of visiting peers is likely to sanction an institution for failing to demonstrate qualities that they know their own campuses cannot. But although the pace is slow, it seems clear that Pew's investment in accreditation is beginning to change the institutional review processes in ways that can only benefit meaningful, faculty-centered assessment of student learning. Because we need good alternatives to increasingly popular state-based testing programs to demonstrate accountability, we can only hope that this progress continues.

Looking Back on "The Year of Accountability"

From Assessment Update *17:5 (2005).*

By late last November, the 2004–2005 academic year had become known informally among higher education policy wonks as "the year of accountability." Probably because of anticipated debates about the Reauthorization of the Higher Education Act (which were supposed to have begun in January but fizzled), no fewer than four major reports on accountability and assessment were issued by various actors between September 2004 and July 2005. While the content of these reports predictably varied, they collectively signaled to the academy that the rules of the accountability game were changing.

First out of the box was the Business Higher Education Forum (BHEF), a nonprofit group of corporate leaders that has become an increasingly active voice in higher education policy in recent years. Their initial report, *Public Accountability for Student Learning in Higher Education: Issues and Options*, was issued late last summer and called on colleges and universities not only to conduct vigorous learning outcomes assessment programs but to go public with the results so that parents and employers could look at them. These recommendations were discussed at an invitational conference at Wingspread in Madison, Wisconsin, which yielded a follow-up report (*Facing Up and Moving Forward: Mobilizing a National Policy Capacity to Address Student Learning in Higher Education*) that reinforced the BHEF's original message but with a stronger imperative for action. In substance, the BHEF report's recommendations were not greatly different from the requirements institutions already face for accreditation. More important was the source. In the past, the BHEF had confined itself largely to topics of finance and affordability—issues apparently more suited to the business perspective. By taking on outcomes, the organization signaled unmistakably that employers are concerned about higher education's performance and that student learning is an essential aspect of that performance.

In September 2004, the National Center for Public Policy in Higher Education issued its third biennial report card on higher education, *Measuring Up 2004*. In addition to the usual dismal story on the affordability of higher education, it contained something new: a report on a five-state demonstration project aimed at addressing the "Incomplete" grade in student learning that had been awarded to all states in the previous two editions. Five states participated in the demonstration—Illinois, Kentucky, Nevada, Oklahoma, and South Carolina (see <http://www.highereducation.org/reports/mu_learning/index.shtml>). For each, the center constructed a learning profile— using data drawn from the National Adult Literacy Survey, existing data on licensure and graduate admissions test results, and the results of two assessments (Collegiate Learning Assessment by RAND Corporation's Council for Aid to Education and Work Keys by American College Testing)—administered to samples of students in representative two- and four-year institutions. In July 2005, the center issued a more detailed report on this pilot effort that included additional analyses of performance gaps for students of color and an analysis of teacher licensure examination results that involved comparing actual test-taker performance in selected states against the nation's highest cut scores for such examinations. The data generated by this project, however, were probably less important than the fact that they were gathered at all. The intent of the project, which was certainly fulfilled, was to demonstrate that such data could be collected systematically if states chose to do so.

The Association of American Colleges and Universities (AACU), meanwhile, was sending a contrasting message through the accountability component of its broad Greater Expectations initiative. In a report entitled *Our Students' Best Work*, AACU argued that a de facto consensus on key general education outcomes already exists among American colleges and universities and that the academy should recognize this officially and get on with the job of providing public evidence that these outcomes are being achieved. The suggested assessment vehicle, as hinted by the report's title, is representative samples of culminating work in the disciplines in the form of senior projects or theses, portfolios, or tasks embedded in senior seminars or internships. A parallel report (*Taking Responsibility for the Quality of the Baccalaureate Degree*) argued that the standards of institutional accrediting organizations with respect to student learning outcomes are similarly aligned and that accreditation should be taken far more seriously by institutions as the main vehicle for responding to growing accountability demands.

Pulling it all together in March 2005, the State Higher Education Executive Officers (SHEEO) issued the final report of its National Commission on Accountability, which had been convened the previous summer. Chaired by ex-governors Dick Riley of South Carolina and Frank Keating of Oklahoma and made up of political, business, and higher education policy leaders, the commission issued a comprehensive list of recommendations aimed at institutions, states, and the federal government. Its report first embraced the recommendations of the three reports mentioned previously in this article, calling on institutions to follow the AACU recommendations and on states to implement systematic student assessment along the lines of the National Center for Public Policy's five-state demonstration project. But the commission went on to endorse other controversial proposals, including those of the National Center for Education Statistics for a national student unit record system to track student progress across multiple institutions and for accrediting organizations to disclose the results of their reviews to the public.

Although some of this barrage of rhetoric can undoubtedly be attributed to the Reauthorization of the Higher Education Act, its scale remains unprecedented. Accountability is clearly in the political water right now, and whatever form it may ultimately take, institutions and faculty need to pay close attention. But cutting across the diversity of these four reports (and they are indeed quite different) are three themes that not only are important but also begin to define a new look for accountability.

First, accountability is now indubitably about *results*. When, as an adviser to the project, I had a chance to review all of the written testimony to the SHEEO national commission, I was struck by how decisively every commentator emphasized that the traditional balance between resources, processes, and outcomes in conversations about accountability had been upset. Even such staunchly resistant voices as the National Association of Independent Colleges and Universities and the American Federation of Teachers led with results and emphasized that evidence of student learning outcomes ought to be the sine qua non of accountability for higher education. Commentators disagreed mightily, of course, on exactly what such evidence should consist of and how it should be gathered. The commission's final report reflected this pluralism by recommending that institutions have a choice of measures within the framework of accreditation while advocating a more standardized approach on the part of states and the federal government. But there is now consensus among all comers that student learning outcomes are accountability's central ingredient—a consensus that certainly was not present ten years ago.

Second, accountability is now far more likely to be cast in terms of *public interest* than in terms of institutional performance. Established accountability measures are overwhelmingly about comparative institutional condition and performance—for example, costs per credit hour, student-faculty ratios, instructional versus administrative costs, or graduation and placement rates. While the "new look" in higher education accountability certainly does not ignore such measures, additional statistics on the benefits that higher education brings to society, state, or region, such as advanced literacy skills among the adult population, levels of workplace preparedness, or voting and charitable giving, are now far more likely to be advocated and included. This additional emphasis is advocated by organizations that are otherwise quite different. *Measuring Up,* of course, begins with population measures, and its impact in increasing broad perceptions of higher education's accountability to the public purpose is clear. When it took on student learning as a category, therefore, it was no surprise that the centerpiece concept was *educational capital*—the sum total of advanced knowledge and skills possessed by a state's citizenry. But AACU's Greater Expectations initiative also puts its consensus list of student learning outcomes in terms of the public interest, emphasizing that these are not just academic outcomes but attributes that are desperately needed for meaningful work and functional citizenship. Meanwhile, endeavors like the American Association of State Colleges and Universities' Stewardship of Place initiative are calling greater attention to institutions' responsibility to connect with and serve the communities in which they are located. This growing commitment to public purposes may have a noticeable impact on institutional data collection, because far too many institutions still don't know very much about the condition of their community or their impact on it.

Finally, accountability processes are increasingly emphasizing *transparency.* Partly, this is a reaction to developments in other sectors—especially the impact of the Sarbanes-Oxley financial disclosure legislation and the recent corporate accounting scandals. For institutions, this implies a demand not only to collect information about performance but to make it public. Again, this is a theme that cuts across otherwise different points of view; AACU, as well as SHEEO and BHEF, are calling on institutions to more prominently display assessment results for public stakeholders. Similar demands for transparency are also beginning to affect higher education's most traditional mode of quality assurance, accreditation. According to a June survey conducted for Council for Higher Education Accreditation, 18 percent of all accrediting organizations (including two of the eight regional organizations) now provide information about the results of individual accreditation reviews beyond simply whether or not an institution was reaffirmed. Another 20 percent plan to make significant changes in public disclosure in the next three years.

It is too early to tell where this heightened rhetoric may lead. The report of SHEEO's national commission contained dozens of specific recommendations, ranging from establishing the aforementioned national unit record database and increasing sample sizes for the National Assessment of Adult Literacy at the federal level to publicly reporting learning assessment results at the institutional level, and it would be unreasonable to suppose that all of them will fly. But some of them will. And perhaps more important, Congress will have a pretty good shopping list to peruse as work on Reauthorization of the Higher Education Act proceeds.

Accreditation in the Hot Seat

From Assessment Update *19:1 (2007).*

Accreditation has without question been the major external driver of assessment for the past decade. Since states began to back off from their initial assessment mandates in the early 1990s amid budgetary shortfalls and a growing fascination with harder-edged statistical performance indicators, regional accreditors have steadily increased the salience of assessment in their successive standards revisions, new review processes, team training, and sponsored conferences and events. More important, the kinds of assessment approaches that the regional accreditors have emphasized are compatible with faculty and institutional values; they are mission-centered, institutionally tailored, frequently authentic, and rooted in individual disciplines. So despite the constant litany of complaint from institutions about "what accreditors want," we simply would not be where we are in assessment today without them.

Given this history, the treatment accorded regional accreditation by the Secretary of Education Margaret Spellings's Commission on the Future of Higher Education (and the Secretary of Education herself) was a bit of a shock. Accreditation was reviled as an ineffective, uneven process that advances the interests of in-groups, gives short shrift to student learning outcomes, and frequently impedes educational innovation and experimentation. Some of these charges, at least in part, are true. But so are the protests from accreditors that they have been misunderstood. Given the importance of regional accreditation to our community and the future of assessment, therefore, it behooves us to understand more fully where both the vehemence and the substance of the Secretary's charges originate.

To begin with, changing the accreditation system is one of the few things among the commission's recommendations that she can do anything about. The current administration may or may not be inclined to significantly increase Pell grant funding, but it is clearly not in a position to do so, given escalating budgetary and political constraints. Implementing the proposed student unit record system also carries a heavy political price and will require congressional action. (In fact, Congress has already expressly prohibited implementation of such a system, so its ruling would have to be reversed.) But regulating accreditation falls within the Secretary's purview through "negotiated rule making." More specifically, the Department of Education (DOE) explicitly authorizes regional and national accreditors to act as agents of the federal government in ensuring institutional integrity, which is why loss of accreditation also means loss of federal funding for an institution. Authorization is accomplished through a body of rules made by the DOE, which can be changed without congressional approval, and is exercised with guidance from the National Advisory Committee on Institutional Quality and Integrity (NACIQI), which the DOE appoints. Changes in both rules and appointments in the coming months can be expected.

What are some of the specifics of accreditation that concerned the Secretary's commission? A big one is transparency. A key element of the DOE's accountability strategy is providing better consumer information in order to let the market drive improvements in the quality of higher education. And information about results and costs are at the center of what parents and prospective students want to know. But the accreditation process tells the public little about quality beyond a given institution's accredited status. To be sure, accreditors are moving toward greater transparency and were doing so well before the commission's report. The Higher Learning Commission of the North Central Association of Colleges and Schools, for example, now publishes a summary of accreditation findings, including explicit strengths and weaknesses, each time it reaffirms a decision, and the other regional accreditors are also contemplating such a move. But the issue continues to vex the accreditation community. A survey of accreditors and presidents undertaken by the National Center for Higher Education Management Systems last year on behalf of the Council on Higher Education Accreditation revealed strong opinions that too much public disclosure would discourage honesty in reporting and would destroy the delicate balance of trust between reviewers and institutions that is considered central to the role of accreditation. In the future, though, there may be little choice.

Another big concern is what's meant by "evidence of student learning outcomes" and how far accreditors will take institutions to task on this matter in an actual review. The Spellings Commission did not, as many still believe, recommend mandating use of a single standardized test. But it did make some pretty strong statements about the need for benchmarked, comparative data on student performance and mentioned a few standardized tests by name. So in rule making, we will probably see attempts to require accreditors to ask for comparative assessment results in their reviews, with more specific guidelines identifying the kinds of methods deemed acceptable. But perhaps more important is an emerging distinction between what accreditors have traditionally required of institutions in the realm of assessment and what the federal government would actually like to see. As we all know (and faculty decry), accrediting organizations require institutions and programs to do assessment. What they do *not* currently do is specify what level of actual student performance on these assessments is good enough. This divide between a process requirement and a performance standard has been emerging for quite some time. For example, two years ago, NACIQI took the National Council for the Accreditation of Teacher Education to task for its failure to establish a minimum pass rate on teacher licensure examinations below which it would not accredit teacher preparation programs. So we will probably also see pressure for accreditors to make more bottom-line judgments about what level of student performance is acceptable, whichever assessment methods are used.

A third area of concern is the perception that accreditation doesn't hold institutions sufficiently accountable and exerts only marginal influence on their behaviors with respect to assessing learning. Certainly, on the face of it, this is massively unfair because much of the now considerable volume of activity in assessment on campuses these days can be attributed to accreditation's influence. But it is equally the case that only recently have institutions been sanctioned in this area and that none have lost their accreditation. And there remain many high-end institutions that still have done little or nothing on assessment, resting content in the belief that they are of such obvious quality that they have nothing to fear. Accreditors have been moving slowly but inexorably to address this situation, but it may be too little too late.

At the same time, there is the perception that accreditation is "inside baseball"—a process run by academics who scratch each others' backs to protect internal interests. And there is truth to this as well, at least in the sense that accrediting organizations are membership-based and so owe their very existence to keeping the goodwill of those whom they are supposed to be holding accountable. Equally apparent is the fact that most institutions don't really meet the letter of most accreditation standards about the assessment of student learning, if these are applied literally. Almost all such standards, for example, specify that learning outcomes be established and assessed regularly for every program and for specified abilities in general education, with results presented prominently to the public. Only a handful of institutions in the country are in full compliance with such standards. In contrast to the other concerns, this is a structural condition—one that cannot be addressed if accreditors remain dually accountable to the federal government and to their own membership. So it will be interesting to see how the DOE tries to square this circle without entirely "blowing up the enterprise," as some Spellings Commission members have advocated.

Regional accreditation is a uniquely American institution, and it deserves our support as a champion of the kinds of improvement-oriented, faculty-owned approaches to assessment that we all value. But it is interesting to note how alien it can appear to respected and respectable members of the academic quality assurance community abroad. As part of an external evaluation of a regional accreditor, for example, I recently solicited a review of a set of self-studies, team reports, and commission action letters from the head of a well-known European review body. Excerpts from his reply are revealing:

"This is all very good stuff from the perspective of an improvement oriented focus, but the perspective that stands to suffer is that of consistency and comparability. . . . Our first [reviews] were conducted along similar lines . . . but our visiting teams had difficulties in identifying the proper criteria for identifying quality. . . . More importantly, our agency could not stimulate the general awareness among the universities of the many problems actually shared among them because processes and reports were too individualistic . . . so we are now applying processes well anchored in the European Standards and with a firm focus on comparability and consistency."

And commenting on a particular institutional case considered exemplary by the U.S. accreditor, he noted "I am surprised that such an elaborate review of the XXX case can leave the reader so unclear on the extent to which standards and criteria have been adequately and precisely documented." Sound familiar?

As of this writing (mid-October 2006), it is too early to tell exactly how this story will end. The Secretary will hold a meeting with stakeholders in late November, which will presumably yield recommendations on how to proceed. And upcoming meetings of NACIQI may well prove revealing. But the handwriting is on the wall that public disclosure of comparable results on student learning—whatever form this may take—will be strongly recommended. So we had better be ready.

Rising to the Occasion: The Alliance for New Leadership for Student Learning and Accountability

From Assessment Update *21:1 (2009).*

It has been more than a year since Senator Lamar Alexander confronted Secretary of Education Margaret Spellings in order to head off her assault on the autonomy of institutional accreditation. Her campaign had begun in the spring of 2006 during the negotiated rule-making process intended to delineate what accreditors would have to do in order to remain recognized as gatekeepers for federal funds. The substance of this dispute centered on compelling the use of "comparable" (and thus, presumably, standardized) measures of student learning outcomes in the accreditation process. This move, in turn, arose out of the deliberations of Spellings's Commission on the Future of Higher Education, which, a year earlier, had argued for the use of standardized tests as a way to discharge accountability for the nation's colleges and universities.

Senator Alexander's prohibition, later written into the Higher Education Act (HEA), seemed to end this contest in the academy's favor. But many of the Spellings Commission's objectives are now being pursued voluntarily by college and university leaders, who are convinced that the academy's accountability challenges are not over. The Voluntary System of Accountability (VSA) initiative launched by the National Association of State Universities and Land-Grant Colleges and the American Association of State Colleges and Universities, which requires the use of publicly reported standardized test scores, is perhaps the best known of these reactions.

There are many reasons for thinking, as I do, that the current accountability bump in the road is not going to disappear the way the State Postsecondary Review Entities and similar draconian provisions arising from the 1992 reauthorization of the HEA did by 1994. First, the importance of higher education to the nation's economy and the individual health and prosperity of its citizens has never been greater. Although it varies across states, the personal income premium for possessing a baccalaureate degree is more than ten thousand dollars a year—noticeably higher than it was a decade ago. Second, we did not live in a "flat" world then. Now, the nation's economy must be globally competitive, and a lot depends on the educational attainment levels of our workforce. But we are rapidly losing ground in this area, according to the latest figures released by the Organisation for Economic Cooperation and Development (OECD). The OECD survey shows U.S. baccalaureate attainment rates for young adults to be only tenth in the world; once, we were first. Finally, business leaders are becoming more strident in calling for colleges and universities to be more responsive to their needs for graduates who are ready to be productive in a twenty-first-century economy, which is putting a premium on advanced intellectual skills. These concerns are echoed by national and state policymakers, regardless of party. For all of these reasons, some of us think that higher education's accountability challenge will continue for a considerable time to come.

With these concerns in mind, about twenty higher education leaders convened in Washington, D.C., in the spring of 2007, with support and encouragement from the Teagle Foundation. They included leaders of most of the One Dupont Circle higher education associations, foundation representatives, and policy people like me who have an interest in assessment. Rather than wait for a new salvo of accountability proposals from federal and state governments, we agreed that the academy needs to formulate a proactive strategy. And the centerpiece of this strategy should be to take visible responsibility for assessing learning and assuring the public that current levels of collegiate learning are sufficient. The result was *New Leadership for Student Learning and Accountability*, a pamphlet published jointly by the Association of American Colleges and Universities (AACU) and the Council for Higher Education Accreditation (CHEA) in January 2008. This document argues that U.S. colleges and universities need to assume responsibility for generating credible evidence of student academic achievement without government bidding, and to put forward a set of framing principles to guide future attempts to do so.

With this foundation in place, the "New Leadership" group met again last September to explore the role and structure of an alliance that could carry this work forward. Members agreed that it is important not to create a new entity that might compete with or overshadow the many initiatives consistent with the New Leadership agenda already being undertaken by AACU, CHEA, and the One Dupont presidential associations. Instead, the objective is to create a critical mass for advocacy and to coordinate efforts among the alliance's members. The organization envisioned would thus consist of only a director and a small support staff.

Participants also agreed that stronger and more active advocacy as well as coordination is needed and that an organization of this kind would be well placed to provide it. First, the group felt that a media campaign is required, centered on op-eds prepared by college and university leaders on the topic of taking responsibility for student learning results. At the same time, participants believe that a parallel campaign should be directed at presidents and provosts themselves, urging them to join the initiative by publicly asserting that their institutions are on board. Second, participants believe that greater communication and coordination is needed among the various associations and research efforts that are joining the partnership. In this vein, participants thought that simple awareness of the many positive efforts going on might provide a basis for responding to future accountability demands.

Efforts to craft the "New Leadership Alliance" are still nascent, but it seems certain that the Teagle Foundation will continue to invest in the idea and that some public gatherings to vet it with the academic community will take place in 2009. But what makes us think they will succeed? Promises to work together on the part of the Washington higher education organizations have not always lasted under similar circumstances. For example, the National Policy Board on Institutional Accreditation—an organization created to remake accreditation entirely in the wake of the 1992 reauthorization of the Higher Education Act—lost steam in 1994 after the new Republican Congress made it clear that it would not fund HEA's provisions and that higher education could sit accountability out.

Are there signs that this new effort will fare differently? I believe there are. First, as is also the case with the VSA, there is an emerging consensus among presidents that a proactive response of this kind is needed. Before the Spellings Commission, they believed that higher education's accountability problem could be cured by a greater dose of public relations; however, the current mood of their external stakeholders has convinced them that something more substantial will be required. If their commitment can be maintained, perhaps things will not turn out as they did in 1994. Second, elite institutions are coming on board. Because the internal economy of the academy is fueled by prestige, it is hard to get any ball rolling if the most visible institutions—those ranked at the top of the U.S. News hierarchy—are not doing it. Arguably, this is one of the most important reasons why assessment has had a hard time getting traction. Tentative elite interest in the emerging alliance can be ascribed largely to the leadership of the Teagle Foundation, whose projects have fostered engagement in assessment on the part of highly selective institutions that would never have given it a thought before. The Teagle-sponsored gathering in September that discussed next steps for the alliance, for instance, had representation from Duke, Princeton, Vanderbilt, and Yale—as well as a host of selective liberal arts colleges.

It is, of course, far too early to predict the outcome of this venture. But I think I can say with confidence that, at minimum, the level and quality of conversation about this important topic will rise in the year to come.

Some Final Reflections

Reviewing two decades-worth of observations about the seamy connection between assessment and external accountability as revealed through my columns is a sobering exercise. On the one hand, for those of us who revel in the intricacies of the political process (I am, after all, originally a political scientist), the wide panorama of state and national agendas and the down-and-in cut-and-thrust of the individual actors strutting their stuff in these struggles remains exhilarating. On the other hand, like any complex political narrative related in the present tense as things are happening, it is difficult to draw compelling generalizations from this body of material. In spite of this, I would like to venture a few.

Spiraling Toward a Conclusion. The events portrayed in the last three columns represent the third major cycle of accountability for higher education performance imposed by authorities outside the academy that I have personally experienced. The first was when the initial state mandates for assessment were enacted in the mid-1980s. The second was when the National Education Goals were put into place and the State Postsecondary Review Entities (SPREs) were established through the HEA in the mid-1990s. Both these waves subsided within a few years with little actually changed. This ebb and flow might suggest a more or less permanent pattern comprised of short bursts of accountability activity within a long term framework of stasis, much like the changing seasons. But I think the pattern is really more like a spiral—alternating changes of condition that lead inexorably in a particular direction—much like global warming. The direction in this case is toward increasingly explicit evidence about student learning outcomes, together with parallel demands for transparent ways to communicate these results to a widening set of stakeholders. If this indeed is true, we should be prepared for more standards and standardization in assessment methods, more ranking and comparative reporting, and increasingly public displays of assessment results. Put succinctly, the "institution-centered" state assessment mandates described in the first section of this collection would never fly today.

Complexity Never Lasts. If the overall conclusion of the preceding paragraph is not welcome for American colleges and universities, my second one may prove more comforting: twenty years of history in accountability for results suggest that complicated and burdensome policy directions like performance funding and mandatory statewide outcomes testing using standardized instruments seem doomed in the long run. Among the many examples of performance funding discussed in this collection, only the Tennessee case has endured, together with the more recent cases of Oklahoma's "brain gain" and the Washington SBCTC's "momentum points" scheme. Meanwhile, performance funding in Arkansas, Florida, Missouri, South Carolina, and Washington have vanished. Similarly, West Virginia, Kentucky, South Dakota, and Oklahoma are now the only states that mandate a standardized test as an accountability measure in higher education. Parallel statewide testing programs in Florida, Texas, Arkansas, Colorado, Utah, and Wisconsin described in these columns lasted only a few short years. Why is this? A probable culprit is lack of sufficient long-term political will to keep big complicated initiatives like these alive. After four or five years, their original political champions in statehouses or SHEEO offices are gone, but institutional opposition to them remains. Added to this is the seemingly inevitable tendency for programs like these to get ever more complicated as time goes on. In Tennessee, for instance, the contents of performance funding guidance documents doubled over time as institutions found and exploited loopholes in the policy and state officials closed them. Evidence like this suggests that, despite the steady march toward more hard-edged accountability for results, many of the nasty things currently being designed and rolled out by external authorities will be short-lived.

Timing is Everything. Tempering both of these conclusions and illustrated by many of the cases that these columns encompass is the impact of the right set of conditions on the fates of state-based accountability initiatives. Foremost among these conditions are economics and party politics. If the country had not encountered a recession that savaged state budgets in 1990, the innovative (and what now seems forward-looking) but expensive COEP testing program in New Jersey might have endured. Similarly, if Newt Gingrich's new Republican majority and its "Contract with America" calling for the reduction of expensive federal programs had not emerged in 1992, we might still have the SPREs and an already authorized "NAEP for higher education" developed for Goals 2000. These examples reinforce conclusions about the fragility of accountability policies that cost money and require a good deal of administrative care and feeding. If a government actor can launch them in good times and implement them flexibly, as Virginia and Tennessee did, they will enjoy a heightened probability of success.

Getting Better at Assessment. Finally, though little noted in my commentary in these columns over twenty years, we have been getting steadily better at doing assessment. This increases the probability that the requirements of any government body or accrediting organization will actually do institutions some good. In standardized assessments, there is less and less reliance on multiple-choice tests in favor of constructed response or task-based problems. The Collegiate Learning Assessment (CLA) is the most visible, but far from the only, example here. Meanwhile, less standardized alternatives like portfolios and curriculum-embedded assessments—always preferred by faculty—are becoming far easier to do because of technology. E-portfolio software is now ubiquitous and almost all electronic course management systems contain subroutines that allow scored student work from many sources to be meaningfully aggregated and analyzed. With the drudgery of authentic assessment reduced through standardization and automation, institutions are in a far better position to respond positively and creatively to the kinds of things that external bodies like accreditors are asking them to do.

Through my association with the National Institute for Learning Outcomes Assessment (NILOA), I recently had the opportunity to write an Occasional Paper that revisited a paper I wrote for the now-defunct American Association of Higher Education (AAHE) in 1987 about the "contradictions" among assessment, accountability, and improvement. While many of the points I made back then remain disturbingly current, I did note that what seemed a stark opposition of assessment for accountability versus assessment for improvement in the 1980s has gradually evolved into a more nuanced "tension." With approaches like portfolios and rubrics applied seamlessly to existing student work, we are now increasingly able to respond to external requests for information about student learning in ways that serve both agendas. In doing so, moreover, maybe we can finally "stop the buck."